Meditation Interventions to Rewire The • Brain

Integrating **Neuroscience Strategies** for **ADHD, Anxiety, Depression & PTSD**

Jeff Tarrant PhD, BCN

Published by
PESI Publishing & Media
PESI, Inc
3839 White Ave
Eau Claire, WI 54703

Cover: Amy Rubenzer
Editing: Donald Altman
Layout: Bookmasters & Amy Rubenzer

ISBN: 9781683730729

Printed in the United States of America.

PESI
Publishing
& Media
www.pesipublishing.com

Acknowledgments

You would think that this would be an easier part of the book to write, but I am finding it one of the most difficult. When I sat down and actually began to consider the amount of support, love, time, patience, energy and reflection from the countless people in my life from all the periods of my life that influenced this work, it is a bit overwhelming. Where do you start and how do you convey something like this in words?

This book is really the synthesis of everything I have been learning from multiple disciplines over the past 15 years (give or take). So, with deep gratitude, I first want to thank all of the teachers, mentors, friends, family, students, clients, & colleagues that taught me, challenged me and supported me… Thank you, Thank you, Thank you!

Specific thanks and gratitude

My best friend and life partner, Erika Patterson. Without you this wouldn't have happened. You supported me, encouraged me and believed in this project when I was skeptical, frustrated, and discouraged.

To my parents, Debbie Kramer and Jim Tarrant, thank you for expressing interest and being proud. It meant a lot and helped keep me motivated.
To my kids, Morgan Patterson and Jacob Tarrant, thank you for keeping me grounded. Whenever my ego would get too involved and I would become too absorbed, you were perfect reminders of what really matters.

To my meditation, qigong, and spiritual teachers (in no particular order), Grandmother Aya, Seido Ronci, Ginny Morgan, Arthur Du, Kenny Greene, Greg McDonald, Ken Cohen, Master Glenn Mendoza, Tom Williams, & Rainbow Eagle, thank you for helping me explore my internal world, connect to something greater, and appreciate the Mystery. Thank you also for helping me learn something of Shamanism, Zen, Vipassana, Taoism, Qigong, Taiji Chuan, Energy Healing, Arhatic Yoga, Kabbalah, and Native American Spirituality.

To my good friend Debi Elliott for facilitating my exploration of consciousness, introducing me to new ideas, encouraging me in this journey and adding a creative flair that has hopefully rubbed off (at least a little).

Thank you to the University of Missouri. I received all of my degrees at Mizzou and worked there in a number of roles. The time I spent working at the Student Health Center with Terry Wilson was particularly important as this experience refined my thinking of many of the concepts in this book and provided a format to teach mindfulness-based practices to the University community. The essence of NeuroMeditation was born at MU.

While all of my students certainly played a role in my education, certain students helped me grow in profound ways. Thank you Molly Menster, Brett Woods, Anna Watermelon, Meghan Keeler, Miranda Walker and Chris Shannon.

Thank you to the neurofeedback community that introduced me to the idea of exploring states of consciousness with technology. Big thanks to all the folks at BrainMaster Technologies and Stress Therapy Solutions. Thank you to Richard Soutar for introducing me to the concept of "neuromeditation."

Thank you to all the students that have attended my workshops. Your attention, comments, feedback, and questions help me clarify and refine my thinking, making the NeuroMeditation program much richer than it would have been otherwise.

Finally, big thanks to the folks at PESI who have sponsored my workshops and published this work. Special thanks to my Acquisitions Editor, Karsyn Morse and Editor, Donald Altman for providing guidance, edits, suggestions, corrections, and clarity. Thanks to Amy Rubenzer for her expert book design and making the brain images work.

About The Author

JEFF TARRANT, PhD, BCN is a licensed psychologist, educator, and speaker. He has devoted his career to exploring and teaching about the mind/body connection. His work utilizes several forms of technology-based therapies including neurofeedback, audio visual entrainment, virtual reality, and heart rate variability biofeedback. In addition, Dr. Tarrant has studied and taught Qigong, mindfulness, and energy psychology for the past 15 years and incorporates these practices into his model of treatment.

Dr. Tarrant is the founder and CEO of the NeuroMeditation Institute (NMI), LLC and provides certification training for NMI therapist and instructors. In addition, Dr. Tarrant is a Global Neurofeedback Initiative (GNI) Instructor and conducts national continuing education trainings on topics including, "Meditation Interventions to Rewire the Brain," and "EEG NeuroMeditation." Other recent works include a series of virtual reality meditations published by StoryUp VR and the book chapter, "Neuromeditation: An Overview and Introduction" in The Handbook of Clinical Qeeg and Neurotherapy.

Dr. Tarrant's research focuses on exploring brainwave changes that occur as a result of contemplative practices, energy healing and energy psychology. He is a regular presenter at national and international conferences and has a private practice in Corvallis, OR where he coordinates the NeuroMeditation Institute.

Author Contact:
www.NeuroMeditationInstitute.com
FB: NeuroMeditation
Twitter: @DrTarrant

Table Of Contents

Introduction

THE CHANGING FACE OF MEDITATION

It's almost impossible to pick up a magazine or turn on the television nowadays without seeing something about mindfulness or meditation. The dramatic increase of interest in these concepts during the past two decades has been nothing short of astounding. When I think back to my early days of practicing meditation (somewhere around 2000), I could find nothing in my local town about meditation and I had never even heard the term mindfulness (granted I lived in a relatively small town in Missouri)! In the bookstores, the topic of meditation was listed under "New Age." It was definitely considered "fringy" or something that hippies did back in the 60's.

How quickly things change! Only a few years after my initial exploration, several meditation groups sprang up in my town. The University of Missouri, where I went to school and taught, has mindfulness-based stress reduction programs available for both students and faculty, and there are a variety of therapeutic groups utilizing mindfulness concepts (e.g., Dialectical Behavior Therapy-DBT; Acceptance and Commitment Therapy-ACT). Mindfulness and meditation has become mainstream. There are programs for kids in public schools, professional athletic teams and Fortune 500 companies. How and why did this happen? How did a 2,500 year old Buddhist practice that was ignored and trivialized in the United States become accepted and embraced in health care?

Partly, we have Jon Kabat-Zinn and Mindfulness-Based Stress Reduction (MBSR) to thank for this cultural shift. MBSR was created in the late 1970's at the University of Massachusetts Medical Center (1990). What Kabat-Zinn did was create a semi-structured format to teach mindfulness and meditation skills to non-Buddhists. He simply taught the skills and concepts of mindfulness outside of a spiritual or religious context. Not only did this make the practice of mindfulness much more approachable to persons unfamiliar or uncomfortable with Eastern traditions, but it also created a clean format for studying the impact of these practices.

In general, MBSR is taught as an 8-week class, meeting two hours each week with a day-long silent retreat near the end of the course. Each class involves didactic instruction around certain concepts and introduces a host of mindfulness and meditative practices including concentration meditation, mindfulness meditation, body scan, movement based practices (yoga), and guided visualization meditations (e.g., mountain meditation). In addition, many MBSR instructors add to, or modify the content slightly to bring in additional practices such as walking meditation, lovingkindness meditations and qigong.

Before MBSR, the impact of meditation practices on physical, mental health and brain functioning was examined by comparing experienced meditators (often Buddhist monks) against a control group. Studies would examine differences in brain structure and function and theorize that the practice of meditation caused these changes. Of course, simply comparing two groups and discovering a difference between them does not actually demonstrate causality. These studies could not prove that meditation created the observed changes. In addition, this type of research did not have a lot of practical application as it was comparing monks with many years of intensive meditation training with persons that had never sat on a cushion—not a very fair comparison! So, while this research is very interesting and paved the way for later research, it did not provide any significant insights about how meditation and mindfulness might work in the general population. In particular, there was no solid evidence for how meditation and mindfulness might help those with diagnosable mental disorders such as depression and anxiety.

MEDITATION WORKS (SORT OF. . .)

One fallacy about meditation and mindfulness is that one size fits all. What we are learning is that differences in how these practices are taught, as well as numerous other factors, can determine the outcome. As a mental health professional, it's important that you understand some of these nuances so that you can be skillful in applying the right meditation and mindfulness tool. Let's take a brief look at what the research has taught us.

With the format and structure provided by MBSR and similar programs, it became possible to study the impact of meditative practices on novice meditators after a relatively brief training experience and the results have been impressive. MBSR has been shown to be an effective intervention for stress, depression, pain, eating disorders, hypertension, hot flashes, general anxiety, panic disorder, insomnia, smoking cessation, sexual dysfunction and more (Lazar, personal communication April 10, 2013). Not only do symptoms improve after 8 weeks of mindfulness training, but the brain changes as well.

A study published in Psychiatry Research, examined a group of meditation-naïve participants before and after completing an MBSR course. Specifically, this study measured the density of gray matter in the brain using anatomical magnetic resonance images. After only 8 weeks, the experimental group demonstrated increased growth in several areas of the brain, including the left hippocampus, posterior cingulate cortex, temporo-parietal junction and the cerebellum (Holzel, et al., 2011). These changes were not observed in a control group.

This type of cutting-edge research is changing the way we think about and understand meditation, demonstrating that even a relatively brief training in meditation/ mindfulness can have a significant impact. These findings along with the popular depiction of meditation in the media may give the impression that "meditation" or "mindfulness" is good for everything and everybody. However, a review of meditation research shows mixed results.

In a meta-analysis conducted by Goyal, et al., (2014), investigators reviewed all the meditation and mindfulness randomized clinical trials that included active controls. They identified 47 trials involving over 3,500 participants. Overall, there was moderate evidence for the use of meditation and mindfulness for anxiety, depression and pain but low evidence of any significant improvement in stress/distress and mental health related quality of life. This study also found no significant impact on a long list of other concerns including attention, substance use, eating habits, sleep and weight. Beyond finding no impact from meditation, there are even some studies indicating a negative response to meditation.

In the book, *The Buddha Pill*, (2015) the authors spend an entire chapter discussing "The Dark Side" of meditation. They reference a range of articles citing negative experiences people have had during meditation including increases in mental health symptoms such as depression and anxiety. In many cases, the individuals reporting negative experiences are those with pre-existing mental health concerns; the exact population that should be helped by these practices.

This is confusing. Why would certain studies have very positive results for certain things, like stress and attention while an examination of all meditation/mindfulness studies show very minimal improvement? And why would certain individuals seem to be harmed by meditation practice?

The reason for this discrepancy in results could be due to multiple factors, including the skill of the teacher, the severity of the clients/students in the program, and the length of participation, as well as the exact nature of the practices used in the programs. **Rather than use guesswork as a clinician,** *Meditation Interventions to Rewire the Brain* **will clearly point out which meditation practices may be better than others for certain individuals, depending on their needs, physiology and how each style of meditation impacts the brain.** Meditation is not "one size fits all."

Imagine you are working with a client with depression who has read an article claiming that meditation helps with mood symptoms. This person begins meditating with the assumption that the optimal state of meditation is a quiet mind. Theoretically, you might even agree that such a meditation would reduce the negative self-talk that often accompanies depression. Initially, the practice seems to help, but then over time your client's depression worsens. The increase in symptoms could be attributed to any number of things, but one would typically not even consider that the meditation might be part of the problem.

Because depression is often characterized by an excess of slow brainwave activity and meditations designed to quiet the mind also increase slow brainwave activity, that style of meditation may be aggravating the symptoms rather than helping. For this individual, it may be better to engage in a meditation that reduces slow brainwave activity and increases fast brainwaves. In this case, the goal is to wake the brain up and help it become more engaged, alert and positive. What clinicians need is the ability to match an individual to the meditative style that will most effectively help them achieve their goals. *Meditation Interventions to Rewire the Brain* will provide you with the tools for doing exactly that.

In a review of meditation research, Rubia (2009) explained it this way:

> What we need is ". . . a more thorough understanding of the neurobiological mechanisms of action and clinical effectiveness of the different Meditative practices before they can be leveraged in the prevention and intervention of mental illness (p. 8-9)."

Rubia's point is important. Essentially what she is saying is that we need a better understanding of how different styles of meditation impact the brain and specific symptoms. It is insufficient to simply say, "mindfulness (or meditation) helps with ..... (fill in the blank). These terms are too broad and generic when we are attempting to use this information to help ourselves or others. We need to get clear about what is happening during these practices so that we can use them to help others achieve their needs and goals. That is precisely what we are doing in this book and in the NeuroMeditation program.

A ROADMAP TO THE FUTURE OF MEDITATION

By examining the current brain imaging research, meditations can be organized into categories based on how attention is directed during the practice, the intention behind the practice and how these styles impact brainwave functioning. The result is a roadmap to the future of meditation. Think of this as a three-part roadmap designed to give you tools for bringing mindfulness and meditation into your clinical work.

The journey starts with Chapter 1: Your Brain on Meditation. Here you will learn in detail about the 4 basic styles of meditation: *Focus, Mindfulness, Quiet Mind* and *Open Heart*. Virtually every meditation practice will fit into one of these styles or represent a combination of these styles. This chapter will define meditation, EEG brainwaves, and how the brain responds to each of the four very different meditative styles. You'll even be introduced to the NeuroMeditation Styles Inventory (NMSI).

The major part of the journey, Chapters 2-6, directly examines these four styles of meditation and considers how and why each one might be best suited for specific mental health concerns. Based on research from multiple fields, Chapter 2 describes why Focus practices may be ideal for ADHD. Chapter 3 explores mindfulness practices for anxiety and stress. Chapter 4 looks at meditative strategies that are helpful for the depressed brain. The Quiet Mind practices in Chapter 5 are vital methods for quieting negative self-talk. Lastly, Chapter 6 investigates how to best work with trauma, even providing a means for intentionally using deep states of consciousness to retrain and reprogram the subconscious mind. Best of all, you will be guided through this process each step of the way with a toolbox of exercises, tips, and strategies to help you find the ideal set of practices for each individual.

The last part of your journey, Chapter 7, acts as a meditative breather and a time for reflection and exploration. You'll gain some additional tips for working with clients, as well as consider how your own journey into mindfulness touches upon everything from peak performance to a spiritual path. My hope is that you'll continue to master and use these tools in your practice and your own life.

Chapter 1 — **YOUR BRAIN** ON MEDITATION

MEDITATION DEFINED

When you hear the word, "meditation," what image comes to mind? For many, the image is that of someone sitting in a full lotus position with their thumb and index fingers touching and a blissful expression on their face. It's easy to assume that the idea behind meditation is to simply feel good or empty the mind of thoughts. But meditation is more multi-faceted than that, and for most people it is a challenging practice that involves a lot of effort, perseverance, and discipline. The concept of the blissed-out meditator is nice, but frequently a stereotype and misconception. But if meditation is not simply sitting quietly, relaxing or day-dreaming, then what is it? What are people actually doing when they say they are meditating or have a meditation practice? The answer: it depends on the type of meditation one is practicing. We can generically define meditation as "a systematic mental training designed to challenge habits of attending, thinking, feeling and perceiving." While this leaves a lot of room for different styles and approaches, it also informs us that meditation is first and foremost a mental training; it is a method or variety of methods designed to shift the brain into healthier and more balanced ways of relating to and experiencing the world. This is important because what we pay attention to and how we pay attention largely determines how we feel, daily behavior and thinking patterns—and thus, the level of our suffering or joy.

MEDITATION DEFINED

"A systematic mental training designed to challenge habits
of attending, thinking, feeling and perceiving."

There are hundreds of different forms of meditation depending on how a person engages his or her attention and intention as well as what tradition the practice comes from. For example, there are meditation practices, such as Transcendental Meditation (TM), where one learns to let go and empty the mind, allowing consciousness to sink into a space of restful awareness. There are concentration practices that ask the practitioner to focus their attention on their breath or an image of the Buddha or a specific word or phrase; gently returning the mind to the target each time it wanders. There are still other practices such as Taiji Chuan that involve a pattern of choreographed movements and a focus on continually "sinking the energy" and "moving like water." All of these can be considered forms of meditation, yet each is quite different.

Because there are so many styles and traditions and there is so much information available about these practices, it is a bit overwhelming. This information overload makes it very challenging for someone to know where to begin or which meditation practices might be best suited for their specific needs. The goal of this book is to simplify this process, providing a practical guide to understanding the different styles of meditation, how they work and how each might be best suited for specific concerns.

Although there are hundreds of specific forms of meditation, these practices can generally be divided into four styles based on the way they impact the brain and how they are asking us to direct our attention. Because specific mental health concerns also impact the brain in relatively consistent ways, we can use this understanding to begin to identify which meditative practices might be best suited for each concern. Throughout the book, this schema for understanding the various styles of meditation will be referred to as "NeuroMeditation."

ARE SOME PRACTICES
BETTER THAN OTHERS?

The research seems clear that all of the various styles of meditation are potentially beneficial, but no one has addressed questions about which forms of meditation are better for certain individuals. For example, are certain practices more helpful for anxiety than others? What about depression or addictions? Some people are drawn toward specific practices and have an aversion toward others. Does this mean that the one's they like are best for them? What about people with different brainwave patterns? Do certain brains respond better to certain practices?

The short answer to this question is that all meditation practices can be helpful. It is unlikely that you will mess something up by choosing the "wrong" meditation style, because there is no such thing as a "wrong" style. It is similar to exercise. All forms of exercise are beneficial, but you get something a little different from running versus weight training versus yoga. In this program, which style of meditation you choose and which practices you focus on will be related to your goals, your personality and the tendencies of your brain.

In the remainder of this chapter, I will explain the role of brainwaves in states of consciousness and how they are impacted by different forms of meditative practice. We will use this information to identify 4 different types of meditation and show how each may be ideally suited to specific mental health concerns. And finally, this chapter will provide tools to help you match specific forms of meditative practice to each individual based on their goals, attentional habits and personality.

MEASURING THE BRAIN

There are an estimated 100 billion cells in the human brain (give or take a couple million). Each of these cells can potentially communicate with thousands of other brain cells through both chemical and electrical processes. This extraordinarily complicated mechanism is what results in our ability to think, remember, understand emotions and plan behaviors. Understanding the basics of how this process works can provide helpful insights into the ways our brain creates and reflects our states of consciousness.

Most brain imaging techniques allow us to picture the physical structure of the brain (MRI, CAT) but tell us very little about the functionality of the brain. Some brain imaging techniques allow us to image blood flow in the brain (SPECT) or glucose metabolism (PET) which can tell us something about areas that are "active." However, these tests are typically very expensive and intrusive. In addition, they require the subject to be in a very sterile and clinical environment, often with bright lights and large noisy equipment around (not exactly the kind of place you would want to study deeper states of consciousness). While research of this type is very important and interesting, there are other methods of measuring brain activation patterns that may be better suited for examining meditative states, which we will explore below.

Communication within the brain occurs through a complex sharing of both chemical and electrical signals among vast arrays of brain cells. Communication between cells typically occurs by sending chemical messengers (neurotransmitters) from one brain cell to another. When a neuron decides it is going to send a signal, an electrical pulse travels through the axon of the neuron ending at the juncture between one nerve cell and another. The electrical impulse triggers a set of events that results in the release of neurotransmitters. These tiny compounds exit the sending neuron and are received by the dendrite of another neuron.

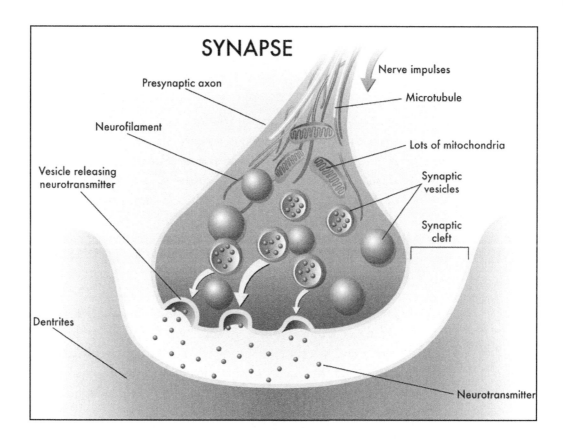

The receiving neuron, taking in chemical messages from hundreds or thousands of other neurons, translates the information to determine its next course of action-either firing a signal or not. The chemicals involved have a range of effects and include the well-known neurotransmitters serotonin, dopamine and norepinephrine. These are the substances involved in psychoactive medications such as Prozac and Ritalin. Clearly, these chemicals are very powerful and can directly influence our state of consciousness. We see examples of this all the time. When people take pain medication or use cocaine, the state of consciousness is being altered by a chemical substance that is changing the behavior of the neurotransmitters in the brain. As of yet, there are no brain imaging techniques that allow us to "take a picture" of the amounts and types of different neurochemicals moving throughout our nervous system at any given moment.

Communication within a brain cell occurs via changes in the electrical current (caused by a change in the potential of charged ions) flowing through the volume of the neuron. Nerve cells are constantly making decisions to "fire" or "not fire" a signal, either enhancing or inhibiting specific forms of communication. When a decision is made to "fire," a cascade of changes in the electrical state of the neuron occurs resulting in the release of the chemicals described above.

UNDERSTANDING BRAIN WAVES

Unlike other brain imaging techniques, EEG technology allows us to measure ways the brain is operating by examining the amount, types and location of various brain waves. This technology has become much more accessible and portable and can be utilized in a variety of environments, making it the ideal brain imaging technique to study states of consciousness.

Every time a brain cell fires, there is an accompanying electrical impulse. These individual impulses are far too small to be read by any standard equipment. However, because our brain is composed of hundreds of thousands of neurons firing hundreds of times per second and in communication with each other, we can pick up any organized patterns that emerge. Essentially, when neurons fire in synchrony, they create bursts of electrical activity. These symphonies of neuronal firing are read by sensors placed on the scalp. Because there is so much electrical activity happening at any moment, the signal we receive is a bit on the messy side. It is messy because it is essentially a conglomeration of everything occurring at any particular moment in a particular region. This pattern is referred to as the raw EEG.

The image on the next page is a screen capture of a 19 channel EEG signal. Essentially, this recording is examining 19 locations on the scalp simultaneously. This is what we see on the scanners in the background of medical TV shows and what most people imagine when they think of brainwaves. However, this group of squiggly lines doesn't mean much unless you are a neurologist or an EEG technician! These squiggly lines are very useful in a hospital setting when looking for gross abnormalities such as a seizure. However, if the objective is to look at more subtle changes in consciousness, this raw signal leaves much to be desired. Fortunately, techniques have been developed to take

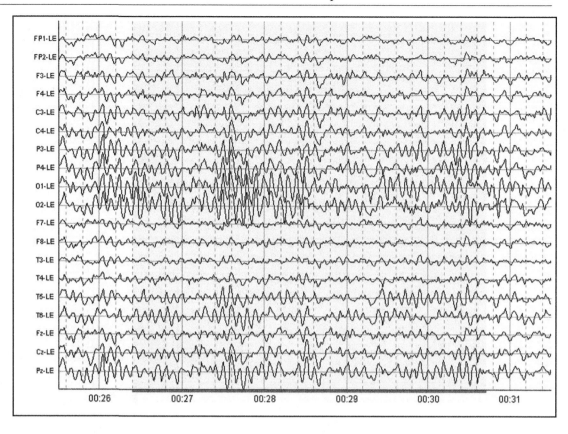

a raw EEG recording, like the one above, and filter it, allowing us to see the different frequencies contained within each of those 19 channels. Making sense of this, however, deserves a more in-depth explanation.

Brainwaves, just like any electrical signal can be described in terms of their frequency and amplitude. Frequency refers to how many repetitions there are of the wave within a second of time, usually referred to as cycles per second (cps) and reported as hertz (hz).

BRAINWAVE METRICS

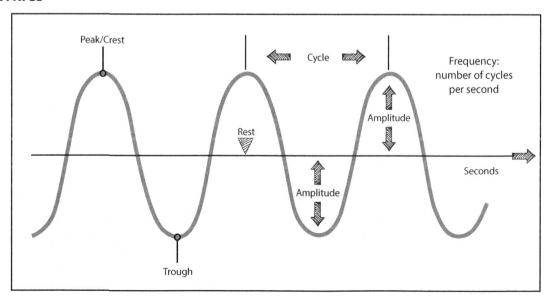

If the image previous represents one second of time and there are two cycles occurring (each peak to peak is considered one cycle), we would describe this as 2 hz activity. At any given moment, the brain is producing frequencies from as slow as you can measure (below 1 hz) to an unknown speed (we are still trying to figure this out). However, the vast majority of brainwaves occur between 1 and 40 hz. Consequently, brainwaves in this range are nearly always the focus of brainwave analyses.

The other dimension of electrical activity that is important to understand relates to power. If speed is measured in hertz and relates to how many repetitions occur in a second of time, power is measured in microvolts and measures how big the waveform is. It is essentially a calculation of the average peak to trough of the electrical signal. On the "brainwave metrics" diagram the vertical (y) axis displays the range of power.

Techniques that quantify the EEG signal, dismantling the raw EEG signal and attaching numbers to it are referred to as Quantitative EEG or Qeeg. Subjects are typically fitted with an elastic cap that contains all the sensors. The cap is placed on the head such that the electrodes land on specific areas, making it easy to compare specific areas between people. After the raw data is recorded it is cleaned to remove any influences that are not related to brainwave activity, such as muscle tension in the face or movement. The remaining EEG sample is then processed through a mathematical formula (fast Fourier transform; FFT) that separates the various frequencies within the raw signal and averages the power of each frequency, giving you a concrete measurement of "how much" activity is happening at different frequencies all over the cortex.

At any given moment, at any point on the surface of the brain you will find electrical activity of every frequency we can measure, from the very slow (1-2 hz) to the very fast (100 hz). That is a bit overwhelming to consider and is typically simplified by creating clusters of frequencies that many people have at least heard of, including delta, theta, alpha and beta.

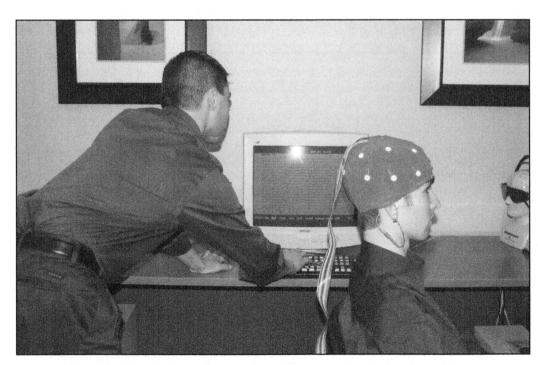

BRAINWAVE BANDS

Brainwave bands are simply clusters of frequencies that are lumped together based loosely on their shape and function.

DELTA WAVES (0-4 hz) are the slowest brainwaves. When they are dominant, the person in question is probably unconscious. Just to be clear, we always have delta activity, but when it increases significantly, it will be very difficult (if not impossible) to maintain any sort of alert consciousness. When this frequency is dominant, the brain is involved in resting and regeneration. Think about what is happening during deep sleep. You might also see heightened delta activity in areas of the brain that have been damaged in some way. Again, it is the brain's way of shutting things down for repair.

THETA WAVES (4-8 hz) are obviously a bit faster than delta, but still very slow. These brainwaves tend to increase while retrieving certain types of memories, in moments of creativity and during the "twilight state" that we experience just before falling asleep. Theta waves are often associated with the subconscious. As such, this is generally the place that people shift toward during a hypnotic state; a state that is more open, creative and suggestible. This also happens to be the dominant frequency for young children.

ALPHA WAVES (8-12 hz) are still considered slow waves although they serve as a sort of bridge between the slower waves of delta and theta and the faster waves of beta. Alpha is like our neutral; our idling speed. Alpha is generally associated with being relaxed and internally focused. For this reason, it is generally associated with states of meditation, although as you will see later in this book, this is a seriously oversimplified conceptualization of meditation and accompanying states of consciousness. Alpha is associated with a quiet readiness. It tends to show up in the absence of stimulation. So, when your eyes are open and you are processing large amounts of visual information, the visual areas of the brain (occipital lobes) show a lot of activity (low levels of alpha). However, as soon as you close your eyes, that stimulation is significantly reduced and those brain regions settle down. In a typical, healthy brain, you will then see large increases in alpha activity in eyes closed conditions.

BETA WAVES (12-30 hz) are fast waves. If you read beyond a basic description of brain waves you are likely to see a whole list of subcategories in the beta category including things like Beta 1, Beta 2, Beta 3 and SMR. For the most part, for our purposes, you don't have to worry too much about those distinctions. Simply knowing that beta waves are fast and are associated with activated states is plenty. When we see increases in beta, it is likely that the person involved is engaged in some level of active processing-thinking, planning, worrying, ruminating, etc. This is the type of brain wave we would like to have engaged when we are balancing the checkbook or working on a project at work or school. Not as helpful when we are trying to relax or go to sleep!

GAMMA WAVES (35-45 hz)   represent a range of brain waves that are obviously very fast. They are generally at the top of the range that you will see in any research on brain training. Increases in gamma waves are associated with a very sharp focus and feelings of creativity, insight and being energized. Bursts of this frequency are often seen during high-level information processing or when various parts of the brain are working together to integrate information. Unlike beta forms of processing, gamma activation is often associated with a more effortless, easy form of understanding, such as we might see during an "aha" moment; effortless insight.

Hopefully, you can begin to see how and why the fluctuations in different brain waves can often tell us something about the person's state of consciousness AND how certain patterns, if they become rigid and inflexible, can be related to certain mental health concerns.

For instance, too much theta without accompanying beta often suggests a brain that is underactivated. This is a brain that may have difficulties doing its job efficiently or effectively. If this pattern shows up in the frontal lobes, the person might have difficulty inhibiting their impulses, sustaining attention or successfully utilizing their working memory. This pattern (excessive theta/beta) is the stereotypical ADHD brainwave pattern. On the other hand, a brain that consistently has large amounts of beta or high beta activity, particularly when it is not needed, may show signs of anxiety, agitation or sleep problems. This is an overactivated brain; one that is hyperaroused.

When people are engaged in specific forms of meditation, you may see increases in alpha in the back of the head, increases in theta in the frontal regions, increases in gamma in left frontal areas, or other combinations of brain waves in specific brain regions. The ways that our brain responds to specific forms of meditation and other contemplative practices provides insight into how these practices may be best used to balance the brain and improve a sense of well-being.

NEUROMEDITATION: DEFINING THE 4 STYLES

Travis & Shear (2010) completed a review of all the published meditation research that examined the brainwaves of meditators. The goal of this analysis was to determine if there was any logical and useful way to categorize or group meditative states based on the impact they have on the brain. While perhaps not absolutely inclusive, they described three distinct categories of meditation practices based on the brainwave patterns they facilitate and the attentional processes involved. The three categories of meditation described by Travis & Shear include focused attention (FA), open awareness (OA) and automatic self-transcending (AST, 2010). Meditation practices geared toward producing a specific emotional state, such as lovingkindness or compassion (LK-C), have historically been considered a subcategory of focused attention based on the observation that these forms of meditation tend to produce the same or similar brainwave activation patterns. While LK-C practices certainly involve a specific focus of attention, they also involve the cultivation of intense feeling states, making them different from more traditional practices of FA (Carter et al., 2005; Lutz et al., 2004).

Not surprisingly, there are also similarities and dissimilarities in the specific regions of the brain that are engaged in each of these practices. Because of its uniqueness, LK-C based practices will be treated as a fourth category of meditation.

The research literature will sometimes use the categories described by Travis & Shear. Other times they will refer to the specific type of meditation (e.g., TM or mantra-based) or they will use other terms such as mindfulness, insight, or Qigong, which may involve a variety of meditative styles. This obviously becomes confusing very quickly. To simplify and clarify the process, we will introduce and use the NeuroMeditation naming conventions throughout the remainder of the book. You will find that these names capture the majority of meditative experiences with straightforward and logical naming strategies.

NEUROMEDITATION DEFINED

NeuroMeditation is the application of brain-based principles to meditative practices.

THE FOUR STYLES OF
NEUROMEDITATION

#1 **FOCUS:** Often referred to as "Concentration" or "Focused Attention" in the research, this style involves the voluntary control of attention and cognitive processes.

#2 **MINDFULNESS:** This style is referred to as "Open Monitoring;" it involves a dispassionate, non-evaluative awareness of ongoing experience.

#3 **QUIET MIND:** Described as "Automatic Self-Transcending," this style is geared toward the automatic transcending of the procedures of the meditation practice and is consistent with TM and Zen practices.

#4 **OPEN HEART:** Sometimes referred to as "Lovingkindness" or "Compassion," these forms of practice generally involve the activation of a positive feeling state and a focus on an "unrestricted readiness and availability to help all living beings"

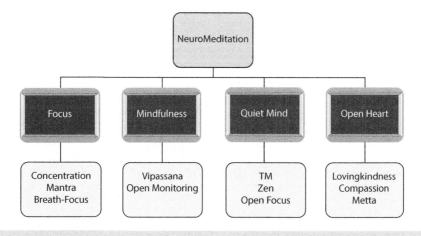

1. FOCUS

Focus meditations involve a voluntary and sustained attention on a chosen object. An example of this type of meditation would include concentration practices that require the meditator to maintain attention on a single object, such as the breath, a part of the body, a strong visual image or a word or phrase (Travis & Shear, 2010). When the attention wanders from this object, the goal is to recognize this as soon as possible and without judgment return attention to the original focus. Studies examining brainwave patterns during Focus forms of meditation have found increased communication between the front and back of the brain in the gamma frequency as well as increases in gamma and Beta2 (20-30 Hz) activity (Travis & Shear, 2010).

Focus strategies may be most appropriate for people struggling with cognitive issues such as attention, working memory or distractibility. If you consider the practice of Focus in relation to ADHD symptoms, the connections become obvious. In Focus practice, you are asking someone to hold their focus in one place, recognize when they become distracted and then return their attention to a single focus as quickly as possible. This is exactly what we want persons with ADHD to be able to do. In addition, the brainwave activation patterns observed in Focus forms of meditation are the perfect antidote for the stereotypical slow brainwave patterns seen in ADHD.

CHOOSING A NEUROMEDITATION STYLE
FOCUS

One approach to choosing a NeuroMeditation style is to consider the specific goals of your client OR their specific concerns. If the lists below are consistent with your client's goals or concerns, Focus practices may be a good fit.

Goals
- Reduce distractibility
- Increase sustained attention
- Reduce mind wandering
- Improve concentration and focus
- Increase self-monitoring
- Improve cognitive self-awareness
- Develop mental stability

Mental Health Targets
- ADHD
- Cognitive decline in elderly
- Mild traumatic brain injury
- Memory problems

2. MINDFULNESS

Mindfulness meditation often does not involve an explicit attentional focus. Typically, it is characterized by an open presence and a non-judgmental awareness of sensory, cognitive and affective experiences as they arise in the present moment. The handful of research studies examining EEG activity during Mindfulness meditation practice consistently reports increases in frontal theta power as well as increased frontal theta communication.

As explored further in Chapter 3, Mindfulness also has a focus component. For example, this focus can be used to intentionally decide where and how to place attention, how to move your body, what to pay attention to, and even to be aware of the consequences of one's actions. This reflective practice improves self-monitoring and executive skills associated with self-awareness, thus it could also be a useful strategy for ADHD, as well as working with cravings, toxic lifestyle habits and addictions.

Mindfulness practices may be particularly beneficial in the treatment of anxiety. Previous research has established that persons demonstrating greater theta activity tend to have lower state and trait anxiety scores (Inanaga, 1998). Not surprisingly, increased frontal theta during meditation has been associated with decreases in both state and trait anxiety levels (Shapiro, Jr., 2008; M. West, 1987). A comparison study, examining the EEG signatures of a Concentration meditation versus a Mindfulness meditation found that the Mindfulness practice resulted in higher levels of frontal theta, suggesting a quieting down of these regions (Dunn et al., 1999).

CHOOSING A NEUROMEDITATION STYLE
MINDFULNESS

One approach to choosing a NeuroMeditation style is to consider the specific goals of your client OR their specific concerns. If the lists below are consistent with your client's goals or concerns, Mindfulness practices may be a good fit.

Goals

- Learning to let go
- Creating distance from thoughts, feelings and behaviors
- Reducing judgment
- Increasing awareness of bodily states
- Increasing awareness of, and regulating emotional states
- Calm awareness of present moment

Mental Health Targets

- Anxiety
- Chronic stress

3. QUIET MIND

Meditations in this category involve moving beyond the procedures of the meditation. Most research involving this style of meditation has focused on the practice of Transcendental Meditation (TM; Travis & Shear, 2010). On the surface, TM appears to be a Focus form of meditation due to the attention being placed on a mantra. However, the actual practice reveals that it is a technique for transcending its own procedures; moving from a state of sustained attention to mental silence (Yogi, 1997). This type of meditation has been studied extensively and consistently results in increased alpha1 (8-10 hz) power and communication (Travis & Shear, 2010). Recall that an increase in alpha1 activity is associated with reduced external attention, vigilance and expectancy (Klimesch, W., et al 1998; Klimesch, W. 1999). This practice is essentially a quieting of the mind and what many people imagine when they think of "meditation."

Quiet Mind protocols may be best for psychological disorders involving disruptions in a sense of self. In the individual with a poor sense of self, quieting the illogical or distorted perceptions of self allows for a broader perspective which is beneficial in the development of a healthy ego. While beneficial for a whole host of issues, this form of practice may be ideal for conditions related to a lack of cognitive flexibility-a tendency to get stuck on certain self-perceptions, conditions such as eating disorders, obsessive-compulsive disorder or personality disorders.

CHOOSING A NEUROMEDITATION STYLE
QUIET MIND

One approach to choosing a NeuroMeditation style is to consider the specific goals of your client OR their specific concerns. If the lists below are consistent with your client's goals or concerns, Quiet Mind practices may be a good fit.

Goals
- Non-attachment
- Quiet the mind
- Minimize internal self-talk
- Non-striving
- Creating distance from the ego-mind
- Restful alertness

Mental Health Targets
- Chronic pain
- Personality disorders
- Obsessive-compulsive disorder
- Substance abuse
- Eating disorders

4. OPEN HEART

Lovingkindness and other compassion-based meditative practices (Open Heart), involve the activation of a positive feeling state and a focus of attention on an "unrestricted readiness and availability to help living beings" (Lutz et al., 2004). Because these practices involve a specific focus of attention and share some brainwave patterns with Focus meditations, Open Heart meditations are sometimes described as a sub-component of Focus practices (Travis & Shear, 2010). For example, research examining changes in brainwave activity of experienced and novice meditators engaged in Open Heart meditations from a Tibetan tradition have shown significant increases in gamma wave communication from front to back regions of the brain as well as increased gamma power (Lutz et al., 2004).

While there are certainly some similarities between the two styles of practice, including the voluntary control of attention and cognitive processes (Travis & Shear, 2010), Open Heart practices are distinct from other forms of Focus meditation in the intentional generation of feelings of caring, love and compassion. Lutz et al. (2006) make this clear when they describe lovingkindness meditations as "the generation of a state in which an unconditional feeling of lovingkindness and compassion pervades the whole mind as a way of being, with no other consideration, reasoning, or discursive thoughts. . .the practitioner is not focused upon particular objects during this state" (p. 540-541).

Open Heart practices, with an emphasis on establishing positive affect and empathy toward others, may be ideally suited as a treatment for depression, grief, and relationship issues.

CHOOSING A NEUROMEDITATION STYLE
OPEN HEART

One approach to choosing a NeuroMeditation style is to consider the specific goals of your client OR their specific concerns. If the lists below are consistent with your client's goals or concerns, Open Heart practices may be a good fit.

Goals

- Improve mood
- Increase empathy
- Increase gratitude and appreciation
- Opening the heart
- Perspective taking
- Increase generosity

Mental Health Targets

- Depression
- Grief
- Personality disorders (empathy)

CHOOSING A NEUROMEDITATION STYLE

As you read through the brief descriptions of each of the 4 meditation styles, the goals of each, and the mental health conditions targeted, you may already have a clear sense of which practices may be indicated for certain individuals.

Most, if not all, of our clients or students are entering into meditation practices because they have a specific goal in mind. They want to be less depressed, sleep better, or have less pain. They picked up a magazine somewhere and read that meditation or mindfulness can help them feel better. If we can guide them toward specific practices that can help them reach their goals more efficiently, doesn't this just make sense?

In some cases, this will be the only criterion you will need to help a client or student identify a NeuroMeditation style. However, other cases are not so obvious. For instance, what if someone does not have a clear diagnosis, is interested in peak performance, or has multiple areas of concern that overlap between NeuroMeditation styles?

If the identified goals and mental health targets for each meditation style do not provide enough clarity, you can ask the client/student to complete the NeuroMeditation Styles Inventory (NMSI). This questionnaire provides a means for clients to more carefully consider their own goals and gain a sense of which style(s) may be best suited for their specific needs. You can find a web-based version of this survey at www.NeuroMeditationInstitute.com under the tab labeled "Learn."

WORKSHEET — NEUROMEDITATION STYLES
INVENTORY (NMSI)

Please rate each of the following statements using the scale provided. Circle the number that best describes what is generally true for you.

Scoring: Items that have an (R) after them need to be reverse scored. For example, if you wrote in '4,' simply change this to a '2' in the space after the (R). After reverse scoring the specified items, simply total each section.

1	2	3	4	5
Never/Very Rarely		Sometimes		Very Often/ Always

FOCUS

1. _____ My mind wanders

2. _____ I am easily distracted

3. _____ I don't pay attention to what I'm doing because I am daydreaming, worrying or thinking about something else

4. _____ I find it difficult to stay focused on what's happening in the present moment

5. _____ I rush through activities

6. _____ I have a tendency to do multiple things at the same time

7. _____ Things have to be very stimulating to keep my attention

8. _____ I get bored easily

9. _____ I have trouble holding information in my mind while I am working on a problem

10. _____ I have difficulty sitting still

11. _____ I do or say things without thinking first

Focus Total _____

MINDFULNESS

1. _____ I find myself running on "auto pilot" without much awareness of what I am doing

2. _____(R)_____ I watch my feelings without getting caught in them

3. _____(R)_____ I am aware of the stories my mind makes up about myself or other people

4. _____(R)_____ I pay attention to physical sensations, such as tension in my body, the wind in my hair or the warmth of the sun on my skin

5. _____(R)_____ When I have upsetting thoughts or images in my mind, I am able to "step back" and observe them objectively

6. _____(R)_____ When distressing thoughts, images or feelings arise, I am able to let them go

7. _____ I tell myself I shouldn't be feeling the way I am feeling

8. _____ I make judgments about whether my thoughts are good or bad.

9. _____(R)_____ In difficult situations, I can pause before responding

10. _____ I have a tendency to get fixated on certain thoughts, feelings, or sensations.

11. _____(R)_____ I am able to shift gears and change plans without difficulty

Mindfulness Total _____

QUIET MIND

1. _____(R)_____ When distressing thoughts or images pop up in my mind, I can let them go

2. _____(R)_____ I like hearing others opinions on a variety of topics

3. _____(R)_____ When I sit quietly, I can easily shift to a peaceful space

4. _____ My mind is constantly providing critical commentary about my thoughts and actions

5. _____ I get stuck in repetitive loops of thinking or feeling

6. _____ I have a tendency to be close-minded

7. _____ My internal state is often agitated

8. _____ I have difficulty seeing other perspectives

9. _____ It is hard for me to relax

10. _____ If I think about something bad happening, I am afraid it will come true

11. _____ I have a difficult time managing unpleasant feelings

Quiet Mind Total _____

OPEN HEART

1. _____(R)_____   I feel grateful and appreciative
2. _____(R)_____   I am generous
3. _____(R)_____   When I hear about something bad that has happened to someone else, I feel sad
4. _____(R)_____   I experience strong feelings in my heart and gut
5. _____(R)_____   I enjoy helping others
6. _____   I have a hard time shifting out of a negative mood
7. _____(R)_____   I tend to see the good in others
8. _____(R)_____   Sometimes I feel too strongly
9. _____   I tend to think of myself first
10. _____(R)_____   I think of things I would like to do for friends and family
11. _____   I am pessimistic

Open Heart Total _____

Overall Totals

Focus = _____   **Mindfulness =** _____   **Quiet Mind =** _____   **Open Heart =** _____

There are several useful ways to use this scale:

a) Section scores greater than 30 may indicate areas that could benefit from that style of practice.

b) You can compare your scores across each style and choose the one or two that are the highest.

c) You can use the scale for self-awareness, becoming aware of some of your tendencies in each category.

d) You can use the scale to measure "progress" as you work with the exercises in this workbook.

MEDITATION TIP — WHAT IF SOMEONE FITS INTO
MULTIPLE NEUROMEDITATION STYLES?

HELPING CLIENTS CHOOSE:

Even though there are several tools in this chapter to help you identify which style may be the best for a particular individual, there will undoubtedly be times when someone seems to perfectly fit into multiple categories. What then?

1. If a client is relatively new to meditation, beginning with a Focus practice is always a safe bet. This is a great starting point and a powerful tool to stabilize the mind.

2. Many meditation practices are a combination of several of the forms outlined in this book. This may be a good fit for someone who does not "neatly" fit into one category. Simply follow a practice that provides multiple categories. Some examples of this type of meditation are provided in Chapter 7.

3. Have your client try a variety of meditations and pick the one that she/he is most likely to practice. All forms of meditation are beneficial. If there are no compelling reasons to stay with one particular form, it may make the most sense to work with a style that has the highest likelihood of follow through for that individual.

4. Develop a plan for having the client try different meditation styles, each for several weeks. Have them pay close attention to the impact of each, and use this as data gathering to make a more informed choice.

CASE EXAMPLE — CHOOSING A
NEUROMEDITATION STYLE

J., a professional man in his mid-40s entered meditation training for several concerns. He noted that he has trouble processing what he reads, feels sleepy throughout the day, sometimes struggles with maintaining attention on detailed information and needs a lot of stimulation to stay interested. These symptoms all suggest an underaroused brain. I considered these concerns in relation to the goals and mental health targets for each style and quickly identified that a Focused practice may be the best fit for this man.

I asked J. if he had ever tried meditation before and he indicated that he had practiced Transcendental Meditation (TM) for many years. While this practice helped him feel more calm and present, it did not seem to help with his other concerns. I asked if he had ever tried other forms of meditation. He indicated that he first learned to meditate by following his breath (a Focus practice). He reported that this type of practice was extremely frustrating, discouraging and unpleasant. In fact, he quit meditating after a short time until he was introduced to TM.

J. completed the "NeuroMeditation Styles Inventory" and received the following scores:

Focus: 32   Mindfulness: 26   Quiet Mind: 24   Open Heart: 36

Based on the cutoff score of 30, J. would seem to be a good candidate for both Focus and Open Heart styles of meditation. However, J. was showing a clear path toward the Open Heart practices based on his scale scores.

ANALYSIS:

J.'s previous experience with meditation tells us a lot about his needs and what his brain needs to find balance. The fact that he enjoyed Transcendental Meditation (a Quiet Mind form of practice) makes sense because this is a very quiet form of meditation-something that would be easy for J. to do given his underactivated brain. J. did not like engaging in Focus practices, such as following the breath because this required a level of concentration that was very difficult and felt "unnatural." While the obvious practice for J. would be Focus based on his reported concerns, he scored highest on the Open Heart form of practice. Because both practices tend to increase arousal in the brain, and J. has already had a bad experience with Focus practices, I began coaching him in Open Heart practices. These worked beautifully as they increased brain activation, but allowed a variety of experience during the practice to keep his interest. J. eventually included some Focus practices into his routine, but we made sure the exercises he chose involved some form of movement to keep his interest and motivation.

MEDITATION TIP

NEUROMEDITATION IS NOT A *"MAGIC BULLET"*

Many clients will approach meditation (and other interventions) with the hope/idea that this will be "the answer." If they can simply identify the right style of meditation, they will have a clear direction and can finally make some progress.

These hopes are not wrong, but they can also be misleading. Many clients and students will be initially excited by the prospect of having a "path," but they have no skill in walking that path and they have not yet put in the time and effort needed to change neuronal pathways or longstanding habits of thinking, feeling and behaving.

It is helpful to remind clients and students that this is a process. Not unlike getting in shape after a lifetime of having avoided the gym. It can happen, but it is often slow and gradual. It can be critically important for the teacher/therapist to act as a supportive cheerleader in the process. Here are a few of the reminders most beginning meditators will need on a consistent basis:

1. **BE PATIENT:** Change is a gradual process. Most people do not feel better after 1 week of going to the gym. You have to go to the gym 3 or 4 times each week for a month or more before you start to notice the improvements and the changes. Meditation is no different.

2. **CELEBRATE THE SMALL VICTORIES:** The fact that the client/student has begun to meditate, even for small amounts every day is huge. Remind them of this. They are taking important steps every day. They can also use an Insight Timer or similar app (see Chapter 2) to track their progress, which can be rewarding.

3. **GET SUPPORT:** It is great to get support from the therapist or teacher, but do they have any friends that can also serve this role? Is there a meditation group they can join or others to practice with?

Chapter 2 — FOCUS MEDITATION:
Strategies for the ADHD Brain

THE UN-FOCUSED BRAIN

Problems with attention and concentration are increasing dramatically in the United States. This is evidenced by the rise in the percentage of the population diagnosed with and treated for ADHD. Recent estimates indicate that at least 11% of U.S. children between 4-17 years of age have this diagnosis. Some states, such as Kentucky, report rates as high as 18.7%. (CDC, ADHD Key Findings, 2014). Sales of stimulant medications have skyrocketed in the U.S., with adults increasing their use at a rate faster than children (IMS Health, cited in Schwarz, 2013).

ADHD AS A
WASTEBASKET DIAGNOSIS

There is a great deal of concern about whether ADHD is misdiagnosed and/or overdiagnosed. These are valid concerns given the number of people receiving this diagnosis and the increased rate of problems. Every researcher and clinician has their own perspective on this issue. Here's mine:

I do believe that ADHD is a "real" thing. You can see it in the brain patterns discussed in this section along with a consistent pattern of cognitive and behavioral concerns AND I also believe it is seriously misdiagnosed and overdiagnosed.

There are many reasons why someone may have difficulties with attention, hyperactivity or impulse control, including medical concerns such as a hormone imbalance. Other mental health issues can often mimic symptoms of ADHD, including PTSD and other anxiety disorders. Children with concerns on the autism spectrum are often labelled as ADHD either before a proper diagnosis is established or as a comorbid condition.

In my opinion, ADHD is also overdiagnosed as there are many children and adults with seemingly minor difficulties with attention that are now receiving this diagnosis (and medications). The diagnostic criterion for ADHD in the DSM-V states that the condition must cause "significant impairment" to qualify for the diagnosis. There is also evidence that the modern lifestyle in North America actually contributes to a lack of attention, hyperactivity and impulse control difficulties. Consequently, there are a number of people with ADHD symptoms caused by poor diet, lack of exercise, restricted time in nature, excessive use of electronics/video games and poor sleep habits. In my estimation, symptoms caused by these lifestyle choices are not the same as a biologically based condition and should not be treated the same.

Whether these numbers reflect the true nature of increased prevalence and incidence of ADHD is up for debate. What is clear is that a large percentage of the U.S. population have concerns about their ability to sustain attention, inhibit impulses and self-regulate and they are seeking the only intervention that is widely advocated: medication.

By gaining a better understanding of what is happening in the ADHD brain as well as through understanding non-medication approaches to brain training, we can begin to offer clients a range of interventions that can effectively assist in improving ADHD-like symptoms without the risk and consequence of long-term stimulant use.

Brain imaging research has found that persons with ADHD (and ADD) frequently have some level of dysfunction in the structure and function of specific brain regions (Castellanos & Proal, 2012; Makris, et al., 2009). The area most consistently implicated in these studies is the frontal lobes (Cortese, S. 2012).

ADHD vs. ADD

ADHD is characterized by a set of symptoms that includes difficulty paying attention, impulsivity and hyperactivity (or some subset of these concerns). When the difficulties are limited to concentration and distractibility, it is often simply referred to as ADD (the 'H' standing for "hyperactivity.") This terminology can often be a bit confusing. I mention this here as the question is often raised about distinctions between those with and without the hyperactive set of symptoms. From a brain imaging standpoint, ADD and ADHD brains often look very similar and will be discussed in this chapter as a single category.

ADHD DIAGNOSTIC CATEGORIES
According to the *Diagnostic and Statistical Manual, 5th edition* (2013), which is the guidebook for all mental health diagnoses, there are 4 possible ways to identify ADHD.

1. **ADHD, Predominately Inattentive Type** (what we would think of as ADD)
2. **ADHD, Predominately Hyperactive-Impulsive Type**
3. **ADHD, Combined Type** (contains elements of both inattention and hyperactivity/ impulsivity)
4. **ADHD, Not Otherwise Specified** (symptoms in this range that do not meet the criterion for one of the other diagnostic categories)

When you consider the functions of the frontal lobes (and especially the prefrontal lobes), it all begins to make sense. Referred to as "executive functions," the tasks of the prefrontal cortex include a whole host of complex actions such as inhibiting oneself, decision making, working memory, problem solving and (of course) maintaining attention. In fact, if you look at a list of problems associated with the prefrontal cortex, it reads like a typical ADHD symptom checklist!

FUNCTIONS OF THE PREFRONTAL CORTEX	**PROBLEMS** WITH THE PREFRONTAL CORTEX
• Attention span • Critical thinking • Perseverance • Forward thinking • Judgment • Learning from experience • Impulse control • Ability to feel and express emotions • Organization • Empathy • Self-monitoring • Problem solving	• Short attention span • Distractibility • Lack of perseverance • Impulse control problems • Hyperactivity • Chronic lateness, poor time management • Disorganization • Procrastination • Unavailability of emotions • Misperceptions • Poor judgment • Trouble learning from experience • Short-term memory problems • Social and test anxiety

THE ADHD BRAIN IS UNDERAROUSED

Perhaps the most common pattern observed in research on individuals with ADHD is a consistent and chronic hypoarousal. This has been demonstrated examining glucose metabolism, brain blood flow and brainwave patterns (Bush, G. 2010). Glucose, a specific form of sugar, provides energy for all the cells of the body (including the brain). The more active the brain, the more glucose it requires. This process is analogous to a car and gasoline. The faster you drive the car, the more gasoline you need. If there is a lack of glucose metabolism, this implies that the brain is less active, which is precisely what we see with ADHD. Similarly, when there is a lack of blood flow observed in specific regions of the brain, there is less activity. Essentially, the ADHD brain (with a heavy emphasis on the frontal lobes) is underactivated. When there is less activity in specific regions of the brain, it is difficult for those areas to do their job efficiently and effectively.

From a brainwave perspective, research has shown that children and adults with ADHD tend to have an excess amount of slow wave activity (theta) in relation to their fast wave activity (beta; Arns, et al., 2012). In fact, the ratio of theta to beta activity in the center of the head has demonstrated a high level of accuracy in predicting ADHD (Monastra et al., 2001). So much so, that the FDA recently approved the NEBA (Neuropsychiatric EEG-Based Assessment) system to measure this specific metric as a screening/diagnostic tool for ADHD.

At first glance this may not make sense. Why would someone with ADHD have too much slow brainwave activity? They certainly look and behave as if they have too much fast activity. Saying things without thinking, moving constantly and being easily distracted all seem like things that would happen with too much fast activity, not too much slow activity. Excessive slow brain wave activity can be thought of as another indicator of decreased arousal, similar to the research describing glucose metabolism and blood flow. If there is too much slow brainwave activity in a particular region of the brain, this is an indication that the area is underaroused and therefore, less able to work effectively.

Based on this functional neuroscience approach to understanding ADHD, we are clearly interested in interventions that will wake up or stimulate the brain (particularly the frontal lobes). When the frontal lobes are running slow (too much theta, not enough blood flow) they are unable to do their job effectively, which largely involves self-management. If you wake up those brain regions, they function better. This conceptualization explains why stimulant medications are often effective for many people with ADHD.

Contrary to the notion that people with ADHD have a paradoxical response to stimulants, the evidence suggests that people with ADHD have a completely logical and obvious reaction. If the brain is understimulated, it stands to reason it would function better under the influence of a stimulant. Not surprisingly, research examining who responds best to stimulant medications is consistent with this model of brain arousal.

Researchers in Australia (Clark, et al., 2002) found that they could predict good versus poor responders to methylphenidate (Ritalin) based on EEG patterns. Subjects with lower levels of brain activation (hypoarousal) responded better! This might also explain why so many people with ADHD seek stimulation in their environment. Engaging in activities that are exciting, novel or risky provides stimulation. During those times of increased activation, the brain is functioning more efficiently. Activities that are repetitive and boring are likely to keep the brain in a dulled state. So, the constant search for something interesting and engaging may simply be an attempt to arouse the brain, giving it what it needs to perform at its best. In this regard, stimulation seeking is a functional "symptom." Engaging in thrill seeking behaviors like extreme sports or illegal behavior brings risks to health and safety, but also activates the brain in a way that feels much more functional. Of course, our goal is to provide the brain with the stimulation it seeks through safe and appropriate mechanisms.

Not surprisingly, many common strategies for helping with ADHD symptoms involve arousing the brain. If you pick up any book offering strategies for managing ADHD, you will very likely see recommendations to exercise regularly. There may be some variation in the frequency and duration suggested, but they will all state that exercise and movement are important strategies to manage symptoms. Why? When you move, you stimulate the vestibular system in the inner ear which activates the Reticular Activating System (RAS) in the brain which is largely responsible for arousal. Movement activates the brain!

With this in mind, perhaps hyperactivity is an adaptive strategy to create arousal. While the person with ADHD may not have a conscious awareness of their behavior, constant moving wakes the brain up by increasing blood flow and the production of important neurochemicals. Use the following worksheet with clients to help them identify strategies for activating the brain.

WORKSHEET — STRATEGIES TO
ACTIVATE THE FRONTAL LOBES

Directions: Under each category, identify 1 or 2 strategies you can incorporate into your life to help turn on your brain.

EXERCISE: Exercise and integrated movements (such as dancing and Tai Chi) stimulate blood flow to the brain, activate numerous brain regions and increase production of important neurochemicals.

_____ Walk to work or school.

_____ Take a walk after dinner each night.

_____ Go to the gym (at least 4 days each week for at least 30 minutes).

_____ Take lessons (dance, yoga, martial arts, Tai Chi).

_____ Stand while working.

_____ Take the steps rather than the elevator.

DIET: The types of food we eat can make a huge difference on how well the brain can do its job.

_____ Avoid simple sugars and simple carbs.

_____ Drink more water.

_____ Eat frequent, small meals.

_____ Increase protein, such as eating some protein every 2-3 hours.

_____ Supplement diet with Omega 3 fatty acids.

_____ Avoid artificial colors and preservatives

SLEEP: Research is clear that getting less than 8 hours a night (on average) increases symptoms associated with ADHD.

_____ Keep a regular bedtime schedule.

_____ Turn off all electronics 2 hours before bed.

_____ Avoid exercising in the evening.

_____ Develop a calming ritual before bed.

_____ Minimize stimulation before bed (extra lights, reading, etc.).

_____ No caffeine 5 hours before bedtime.

_____ Keep the temperature low.

_____ Consider natural relaxants such as chamomile tea and or lavender essential oils.

_____ Spend time outdoors in sunlight especially at dawn and dusk.

NOOTROPICS FOR
INCREASED FOCUS

During the last several years there has been increasing interest in drugs, supplements and other substances that are designed to improve cognitive functions. These products are generically referred to as nootropics and claim to assist in a variety of executive functions such as attention, memory, creativity and motivation. Some nootropics are simply stimulant medications such as Ritalin and Modafinil. However, another class of nootropics include plant based, naturally occurring substances that have been shown to assist in a variety of cognitive functions. These products generally include a combination of well-known botanicals such as Ginkgo Biloba, L-Theanine and L-Taurine.

One such product that has recently caught my attention is called Mastermind™ produced by a company called Allysian Sciences. Not only do they use organic and GMO-free ingredients, but there is also some preliminary research to back up their claims of improved cognitive skills.

In a randomized, doubled-blind study comparing Mastermind™ to a placebo, it was discovered that the Mastermind™ group demonstrated a 15.6% increase in working memory capacity as well as a 9.9% improvement in working memory speed after a 30 day trial. In addition, these improvements were not shown in the placebo group.

To examine the impact of this nootropic on brain functioning, I conducted a Quantitative EEG on someone that had never used Mastermind™, before and then 45 minutes after taking the suggested dose. I examined the change in 5 brainwave patterns (delta, theta, alpha, beta and gamma). The results indicated a significant decrease in slow brainwave activity. In fact, the slowest brainwaves decreased the most, whereas the fastest brainwaves did not change much at all. It was also noted that the majority of the change was in the frontal lobes. The overall impact of this pattern is that the brain-especially the frontal lobes- became more activated after Mastermind™.

Changes in Delta Brainwaves

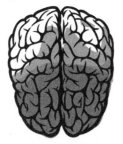

Changes in Gamma Brainwaves

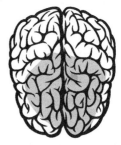

Note: white colors indicate no change. Grey colors indicate a decrease of activity. The deeper the color, the more change.

LAVENDER AND VETIVER

Essential oils are volatile aromatic liquids that are distilled from the various parts of plants (seeds, bark, leaves, stems, flowers, etc.). The specific constituents of the oil determines its impact on the mind and body. Some of these constituents are able to cross the blood-brain barrier and directly impact nervous system functioning. In fact, certain essential oil constituents, such as the sesquiterpenes, are known to specifically interact with neurotransmitters including glycine, dopamine and serotonin (Wang et al., 2012; Okugawa et al., 2000).

Based on this, it should not be surprising that there has been research looking at the use of essential oils for mental health concerns. Two essential oils stand out as having a potential benefit for ADHD related symptoms:

In one study, researchers compared the impact of two different essential oils on EEG activity, alertness, mood and performance on a series of math problems. Subjects were assessed before and after a 3 minute exposure to either lavender or rosemary aromatherapy. After the aromatherapy, the lavender group showed increased beta brainwave activity, improved mood, feeling more relaxed and improved their speed and accuracy on the math task (Diego, et al., 1998).

In a case study comparing Vetiver, Cedarwood and Lavender for ADHD children, it was discovered that all of the oils led to improved performance on a CPT, although Vetiver showed the strongest improvement (followed by Cedarwood and Lavender).

In a small study conducted by this author, 7 children with ADHD symptoms were given Lavender essential oil and instructions to use it 3 times each day for a 2 week period. They were assessed on parent and teacher behavior rating scales and a computerized test of attention. After the 2 week trial, 3 of the subjects showed significant positive changes on 10 or more measures, 3 of the subjects showed positive changes on 3-5 measures and 1 subject showed no significant improvement. The behavior checklist areas that showed the most improvement were: attention problems, hyperactivity, conduct problems, depression and adaptability.

There is evidence that strategies such as sleep and diet both influence brain arousal and can have a significant impact on ADHD symptoms. While lifestyle changes are important strategies, none of them directly strengthen neural circuitry or specifically develop skills of attention and impulse control, which is our primary focus. To develop specific skills in specific brain regions, you have to directly exercise them.

SHAPING THE BRAIN: THE STORY OF BRAIN PLASTICITY

The cover story of *Newsweek* January 9 & 16, 2012, was an article titled, "31 Ways to Get Smarter-Faster." It was largely focused on how to improve cognitive functioning. One of the experts interviewed for the story was Harvard psychologist Steven Pinker. In response to the question, "how do you buff your brain," Dr. Pinker stated,

> *"No gimmicks. If you want to get a lot out of reading, read a lot; if you want to get better at remembering errands or birthdays, practice remembering errands or birthdays. No shortcuts, no cross-training-no Sudoku."*

While this statement may be a little strong, Dr. Pinker is making an important point. The most direct and efficient way to improve specific cognitive skills is to practice those specific skills. If you want to get better at reading, practice reading. If you want to get better at remembering errands or birthdays, practice remembering errands or birthdays!

Applying these ideas to our current area of interest, the best way to improve attention and reduce mind wandering is to practice sustaining attention and recovering quickly from distractions! Focus forms of meditation provide this practice.

FOCUS NEUROMEDITATION

Focus forms of meditation involve voluntary and sustained attention on a chosen object. An example of this type of meditation would include concentration practices that require the meditator to maintain attention on a single object, such as the breath, a part of the body, a strong visual image or a word or phrase (Travis & Shear, 2010). When the attention wanders from this object, the goal is to recognize this as soon as possible and without judgment return attention to the original focus. Focus meditation is training your brain to pay attention and be less distracted! In fact, in many meditative traditions this form of meditation is often used as a starting point to "stabilize the mind." As such, it is the perfect intervention for persons with attentional difficulties such as ADD or ADHD and there is research to support this idea!

Numerous studies have investigated whether meditation and mindfulness practices improve cognitive functioning. Overall, the studies examining the impact of a time-limited or short term practice show mixed results; some seem to suggest that a minimal amount of practice has a significant and positive impact, while others do not. However, a very clear and consistent finding is that long-term meditators and meditators that spend more time practicing, clearly show improved cognitive performance on a number of performance measures compared to control groups (Chiesa, 2010).

WORKSHEET — EXERCISING THE
FRONTAL LOBES IN DAILY LIFE

There are many popular computerized cognitive training programs and games available to improve attention, working memory and concentration. These games are useful tools, but do not replace the power of practicing skills in "real life." Below are some ways to strengthen frontal lobe skills throughout your day. Choose one or two to begin practicing right now.

_____ Remember the names of people you meet.

_____ Pay attention to what others are saying when they talk to you (Avoid planning what you will say in response).

_____ Notice the trees and houses as you walk or drive to work.

_____ Reduce distractions in your environment; do one thing at a time.

_____ Challenge yourself to remember the items on your grocery list or exactly where you parked your car.

_____ Next time you eat out or get your hair done, calculate the tip in your head rather than using a calculator or "cheat sheet."

_____ Before bed, recall as many details of your day as possible.

_____ Pick a daily activity to become completely engrossed in, allowing it to absorb your entire attention.

WORKSHEET — **HOW DISTRACTED ARE YOU?**

For this exercise, you will need a piece of paper, pencil and timer.

1. Find a comfortable position where you can sit without disruption for a few minutes at a table or desk.

2. Hold the pencil over the paper somewhere near the top 1/3 of the page.

3. Set the timer for 3 minutes.

4. Close your eyes and attempt to empty your mind.

5. For each thought you notice, place a hash mark on the page

Questions for Further Consideration:

Do you think you caught every thought that occurred?

Is awareness of a bodily sensation a thought?

How many of your thoughts were the same thought repeating itself?

Were the thoughts coming quickly? Slowly? As images? Words?

The point of the exercise is not to prove anything. Simply becoming aware that the mind is very busy is important and is a way of paying attention.

FOCUS **BASICS**

While there are many different traditions and styles representing a Focus or concentration practice, the format is relatively straightforward and consistent among traditions.

1. Place your attention on an object
   (breath, candle flame, flower, mantra).

2. Hold your attention on the target.

3. Recognize when the mind wanders.

4. Promptly return the focus to the object of your attention.

A few studies have attempted to compare the impact of Focus and Mindfulness practices, but these studies all have significant limitations. One difficulty in comparing the two styles head-to-head lies in the fact that in many traditions, Focus practice is often considered a "prerequisite" to Mindfulness practice. The idea being that it is important to stabilize the mind before you add any additional attentional tasks. Further complicating matters, Focus practices are actually a component of the Mindfulness experience (Lutz, 2015), making it difficult to clearly separate the influence of the two styles. Despite these difficulties, some research is suggesting that even a relatively short-term practice can have a significant impact.

Jha and colleagues (2011) examined the impact of an 8-week mindfulness training on persons naïve to meditation. The emphasis of the class was on Focus practices. After 8 weeks, they found that the participants showed significant improvements in orienting attention. To address the concern that perhaps it is simply the stress reduction that is improving attention (and not necessarily the meditative component) another study compared randomly assigned students to either an 8-week mindfulness-based stress reduction class (MBSR) or an 8-week non-mindfulness stress reduction class.

These researchers also offered financial incentives to some of the students to see what role motivation might play. The authors reported that the MBSR group showed significantly improved performance on selective attention compared to all other groups. So, while we still need additional research in this area to fully understand the role of mindfulness and Focus meditations on attentional processes, it seems clear that even a relatively short period of training and practice can lead to significant improvements.

FOCUS MEDITATION AND BRAINWAVES (THE TECHNICAL STUFF)

Despite some of the early thinking that meditation only involves increasing alpha brain waves, there is now clear evidence that certain types of meditation have a very different impact on brain functioning. Rather than increasing "slow" activity (alpha), they increase fast activity (beta2 and gamma).

The Travis and Shear study mentioned in Chapter 1 found that meditation practices that had a concentrative element showed consistent patterns of brain activation; specifically, increasing frontal-parietal gamma coherence and power as well as increasing Beta2 power (20-30 Hz; Travis & Shear, 2010). Doesn't this make sense given the skills involved in a Focus meditative practice? We are asking our minds to be actively engaged and focused on one thing. Knowing what brain waves are involved is only part of the equation to understanding the impact of a Focus style meditation. It is also important that we understand what regions of the brain are involved.

Because attention is complex, multifaceted, involves several areas of the brain and at least two different networks (Petersen & Posner, 2012), it is difficult to simply identify one area of the brain that may be "the most" important or involved in Focus meditations. While it is nice to see research showing activation of the frontal and parietal lobes, these are very large areas of the cortex (the outer-most layer of the brain). Other meditation brain imaging research has shown that a variety of deeper brain structures may be involved in a Focus practice.

Research conducted by Lehmann et al., (2001) demonstrated that different brain regions are activated depending on the specific focus of the practice and the type of concentration engaged. If the target of attention was something visual, visual centers were engaged. If the target was verbalization of a mantra, verbal areas were activated and when the meditator focused attention on the dissolution and reconstitution of the self, frontal areas were activated. Despite these observed differences, all Focus practices have something in common. They all require sustained attention and re-orientation after episodes of mind wandering. This is true whether the specific focus of the meditation is the flow of breath, an image of a deity or the flow of Qi around the body.

One brain area that is consistently involved in tasks requiring self-regulation of cognition and emotions is the Anterior Cingulate Cortex (ACC). This region of the brain shows increased activation during tasks that require selective attention or inhibiting a response (Crottaz-Herbette & Menon 2006), which is precisely what is required during a Focus meditation. Additional support for the role of the ACC can be found in lesion studies showing that dysfunctions in this brain region lead to executive and attention deficits (Cohen, Kaplan, Moser, Jenkins, & Wilkinson, 1999; Ochsner et al., 2001; Swick & Turken, 2002).

The ACC has also demonstrated different connectivity patterns depending on the sensory modality of the attention task involved. (Crottaz-Herbette & Menon, 2006). What this means is that it doesn't necessarily matter what the focus of attention is (breath, mantra, visualization), the ACC is going to be involved in holding the attention. Consequently, the ACC is going to be a central player in all Focus meditation tasks regardless of the specific target of meditation.

Sustaining attention, a critical component of Focus styles of meditation is made difficult by the mind's tendency to drift or become distracted, referred to as "mind wandering." An examination of brain regions involved in mind wandering consistently implicates the Default Mode Network (DMN; Buckner, 2008; Mason, Norton, & Horn, 2007). This area of the brain is discussed in further detail in Chapter 5, but typically becomes more active in the absence of any external, goal-oriented activity. Activation of the DMN is basically associated with self-referential thought. What this means is that when we are focused on something, the DMN is quieter. As soon as we let go of our focus, we begin thinking about ourselves (or something in relation to ourselves) at which point the DMN kicks into gear. In this way, the DMN is associated with mind wandering.

FOCUS NEUROMEDITATION AND THE BRAIN
THE RESEARCH

- In a study comparing novice and expert meditators during a concentration meditation practice, fMRI brain imaging showed that several areas were involved in the maintenance of focused attention (Brefczynski-Lewis, Lutz, Schaefer, Levinson, & Davidson, 2007); these included:

  o the dorsolateral prefrontal cortex (involved in monitoring)
  o the visual cortex (engaging attention) and
  o the superior frontal sulcus and intraparietal sulcus (attentional orienting)

- Lehmann et al. (2001) found increases in gamma activity in an advanced meditator that shifted brain areas depending on the type of processing involved. When the Buddha was visualized, visual centers were activated. When the focus was the verbalization of a mantra, verbal areas were activated and when he concentrated on dissolution and reconstitution of the self, frontal areas were activated.

- Numerous studies have shown increased beta and/or gamma activity during Focus meditation practices, including Loving kindness/compassion, Qigong, Zen-3rd ventricle, and Diamond Way Buddhism (Huang & Lo, 2009; Lehmann et al., 2001; Litscher et al., 2001; Lutz et al., 2004).

BRAIN REGIONS INVOLVED IN
FOCUS MEDITATION

Anterior Cingulate Gyrus (or Anterior Cingulate Cortex)

This region of the brain serves as a connection between the higher brain centers of the cortex and the lower brain centers of the limbic system. As such, it is very important in coordinating elements of thinking and feeling. The ACC is involved in many tasks, one of which is the ability to hold attention on a single object.

The Posterior Cingulate Gyrus (or Precuneus)

This region is the hub of the Default Mode Network (DMN). This region of the brain is very much involved in thoughts that are related to our idea of self (which is pretty much all of our thoughts). In this way, this region is important in mind-wandering.

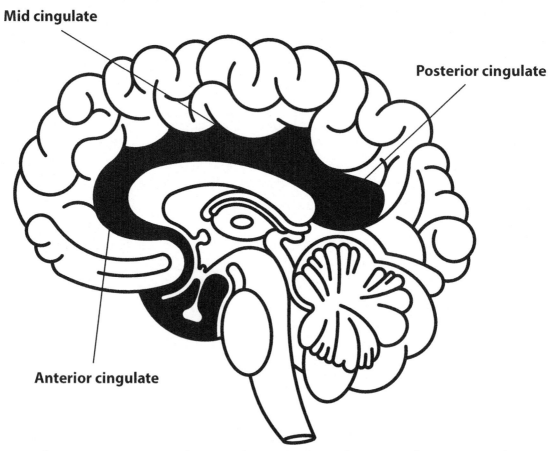

Focus meditation practices involve switching activation between the ACC and the DMN. When the mind is not on a task (function of ACC), it is thinking about the self (DMN).

Let me provide an example of how this might work in a daily experience. If you are working on a project and your attention is on this task, your DMN will be "off." As soon as you take a break, the mind immediately shifts away from the task and begins doing other things. What does it do? In general, it starts thinking about the state of itself, "I'm hungry," or "I wonder what is on TV tonight" or "what time do I have to be at work tomorrow." Whatever the thought, it is very likely about you (self-referential). Even if you are thinking about your kids or your partner or your parents, you are thinking about them in reference to you, at which point the DMN is turned "on."

Perhaps you can see how this might play out in the context of a Focus meditation. When engaging in a Focus meditative practice, the task is to hold the mind in one place during which time the DMN is "off." The mind inevitably drifts off-task onto some other task or topic, which is nearly always linked to some aspect of self and increased activation of the DMN.

So. . . sustained attention, like the type that occurs during a Focus meditation is typically not a single state, but a fluctuation between focused attention and mind wandering (Hasenkamp & Wilson-Mendenhall, 2012).

In addition to the roles in attention processing already noted, the ACC becomes more active during awareness of mind wandering (Craigmyle, 2013). During a Focus meditation, activation patterns are repeatedly shifting back and forth from the ACC to the DMN and then back again as the mind shifts from being focused to distracted.

Keeping it Real: Tips, Tools, Strategies and Aids

As you have been reading and considering the material in this section, you may have wondered about the practicality of asking someone with significant attention-based difficulties to sit and keep the mind focused on one thing. Isn't this setting someone up for failure? Asking them to do the very thing that may feel impossible for them! For years, I made that assumption. I believed that if someone had ADHD or similar difficulties there was no point in asking them to engage in meditation. However, once I began exploring this with clients, I found that many of them were not only receptive to the idea, but actually enjoyed the practice. I think this is important to remember.

At the same time, there are also clients who resist the practice or feel that they simply cannot do it and are therefore unwilling to try. A subgroup of the resistant clients have attempted to meditate in the past and had some sort of failure experience. Usually, these "failures" are related to having unrealistic expectations about what meditation looks and feels like and the amount of time required to get any benefit. For these clients, it is important to offer additional information, tips, strategies and aids to assist them in initiating and maintaining a meditation practice.

SCRIPT — FOCUS
MEDITATION

Begin by tuning in to your posture. What would it look like if you were sitting in a state of alert relaxation? Keep the back straight, sitting up straight and tall but without any unneeded tension in the body. Keep the head perfectly balanced on the neck and torso, making sure that you are not "looking up" or "looking down." The eyes can remain slightly open or closed if that is easier. Which way will help you to maintain a level of focused attention? Place the hands comfortably, one hand over the other with thumbs lightly touching, holding this hand posture just in front of the navel. (This is known as a traditional "mudra," or a ritual hand position used in Eastern meditation). Can you feel how you are sitting with dignity?

Shift your attention to the breath. Allow your breathing to be relaxed and natural. Choose a way to focus on the breathing by noticing bodily sensations. Maybe you focus on the movement of the belly, expanding with each inhale and contracting with each exhale. Maybe you focus on the feeling of the air moving through your nostrils. Cool air moving in with each inbreath. Warm air moving out with each outbreath. Choose a single point of focus for this meditation and hold your attention there. . ..

Gently and quietly count each breath cycle. Inhaling and exhaling, this is one. Inhaling and exhaling, this is two. Continue watching the breath and counting until you reach number 10. Return to number 1 and continue the process. When the mind wanders and you lose track of the number, simply return the focus to the breathing without judgment and begin counting again at number 1. There is no "good" or "bad." It is simply practice. Whatever happens and however the mind behaves, this is simply information.

Modification: Rather than focusing exclusively on the feeling of the breath moving in and out of the nostrils or the abdomen contracting and expanding, you can tie the breath to an energetic point in the body. Because of the intent of this practice, it might be useful to focus on the front of the brain, imagining breathing energy and bright light into the front of the brain on each inhalation. With each exhalation, imagine that energy soaking in and settling deep into the brain. Imagine that the light brings with it healing and increased activation, it is, as if you are activating and turning on the brain with each breath.

FOCUS MEDITATION TIP #1
LENGTH OF PRACTICE

Many beginning meditators have the idea that it is necessary to sit for 30 minutes to get any results. This belief is a setup for failure. In the beginning, very few people can sit and meditate for more than a few minutes. If they do sit for 30 minutes they are very likely taking a nap, relaxing or chasing thoughts and memories. This time may be enjoyable and relaxing but it is not meditation. Instead, begin with success in mind.

1. **Be Realistic**

   Start with 3-minute mini-meditations. After a week or so, extend the time to 5 or 7 minutes. Gradually increase the amount of time until you can semi-comfortably complete a 20-25 minute meditation. 3 minutes of meditation is better than zero minutes!

2. **Be Patient**

   Allow yourself time to develop stability of mind. Meditation is a skill that requires work. It takes a lot of practice and is often uncomfortable. The most important thing is to practice, try not to judge the quality of the practice.

3. **Be Practical**

   Mange your mental awareness of time by using a timer. Smart phone applications such as the Insight Timer will ring a meditation bell for you at the beginning and end of the meditation cycle. This allows you to predetermine the length of the meditation and then, as much as possible, let go of the time focus. You do not need to count the minutes; your timer is doing that for you. The time remaining can be a huge distraction and this is one tool that may help let go of that particular concern. In addition, various versions of this phone app allow you to track your practice, which can also be a nice incentive!

If you type "meditation timer" into the search of your smart phone, you will see several options, most of which are free and very similar in function.

FOCUS MEDITATION TIP #2
POSTURE

1. Choose a Comfortable Spot

This may be a traditional meditation cushion (zafu), but it can also be a chair. Do not lie down. Lying down signals the brain that it is time to go to sleep and often results in a deeper, more relaxed state of consciousness than we are looking for in this practice. For the same reason, it is generally best to avoid practicing on your bed.

2. Relaxed and Alert

Find a posture that conveys the state of consciousness you are seeking-relaxed and alert. What does that look like in your body? What would it look like if you were sitting with dignity? If the mind becomes drowsy during practice and it is difficult maintaining awareness, consider raising the arms while you are sitting or standing up during your meditative practice.

3. Hand Placement

Choose a hand placement that will facilitate this state of mind. The hands resting on the knees might be comfortable, but can also lend itself to a slumping posture, which leads to a slumping mind! It might be better to place one hand on top of the other, both palms up with the thumbs lightly touching in a traditional meditation mudra. This hand position is typically held in front of the navel. The act of holding the arms and hands in this posture makes it difficult to become "too relaxed." In addition, the pressure of the thumbs pressing against each other can be used as a form of feedback. When we are overly focused and engaged in some sort of story or memory, the thumbs will tend to press too hard. When we are drifting and the mind is unfocused, the thumbs tend to drift apart.

4. Head

Keeping the head level can be another source of feedback. When we are "in our heads" the chin tends to drift upward as if you are looking toward the sky. When the mind becomes sleepy or unfocused, the posture tends to slump forward and the chin begins to move toward the chest.

5. Eyes

The eyes can be open or closed. Explore for yourself and figure out which of these states will help you keep the mind focused. Some people become more distracted by internal information while others are more distracted by external information.

FOCUS MEDITATION TIP #3
DO NOT SHIFT FOCUS

When engaged in a Focus form of practice, it is very common and tempting to begin with the attention on the breath, perhaps deciding to focus on the sensation of the belly expanding and contracting with each inhalation and exhalation. After a few moments, it seems to make more sense to shift to watching the breath by examining the flow of air through the nostrils, noticing the cool air coming in and the warm air coming out and then a few moments later it seems like an even better idea to shift your attention to the center of your forehead.

While it is certainly useful to find a point of focus that will aid in your ability to stay on task, it is not useful to keep changing that focus. This is essentially following the minds tendency to continuously seek stimulation. In essence, the mind becomes bored and is looking for something more interesting.

Don't fall for this trick. When you notice a tendency to want to change your focus, acknowledge this, recognize it as the mind seeking stimulation and return to your original point of focus.

In this way, you will teach the mind stability and consistency.

FOCUS MEDITATION TIP #4
CHOOSING A FOCUS

For a Focus practice, the actual object of attention is less important than having a single focus. However, there are some general guidelines that may be helpful in selecting a focus.

The Breath

Many traditions use the breath as a point of focus. This is convenient since you always have it with you, offers several aspects to work with and concurrently provides an element of mindfulness (you are paying attention to what is happening with yourself in the moment). Here are a few ways you can focus your attention on the breath:

- Observe the movement of the air as it moves in and out the nostrils. Notice the temperature change when you inhale versus the exhalation. Notice if the air moves more easily and smoothly through one nostril versus the other.

- Observe the expansion and contraction of the belly/torso/chest. We will discuss the value of belly breathing in chapter 3. For this practice, the key is to be aware of the movement with each breath.

- Follow the path of the breath, by mentally visualizing the breath moving through the nose, down the trachea and into the lungs with each inhalation. Reverse the path, mentally following it for each exhalation.

- With each breath, imagine breathing light or healing energy into a specific part of the body (brain, heart, lungs, third eye, etc.). With each exhalation, imagine sinking this energy into the body area.

External Object

For some people, it is more effective to focus the attention on an external object. Generally, this should be something that is neutral, has intrinsic beauty or meaning to the meditator. Examples include:

• Candle flame

• Flower

• Statue or picture of religious/spiritual figure

• Spiritual symbol

• Mandala

You generally, do not want to choose something that will lead the mind to become more engaged-analyzing, imagining, interpreting, etc.

Mantra

A mantra is simply a word or phrase that is repeated over and over as a way to stabilize the mind. This word or phrase can be in the meditators language of choice. It can be something designed and created by the meditator, taken from a spiritual/religious tradition, or a specific intention. The mantra can be coordinated with the breath cycle or not. Examples of specific mantras:

• "Om Mane Padme Hum"

• Breathing in "I am safe," breathing out "I am calm"

• "I am, that I am"

• "All is love"

• "One"

• "Peace"

USE THE BODY

Engaging the body in Focus forms of practice may be important for at least two reasons. First, engaging the body activates the brain. Standing, balancing and movement all lead to significant increases in brain activation patterns. Because this is precisely what we are attempting to encourage with this style of practice, adding the body can make the practice much more engaging.

In addition, there is abundant evidence that physical exercise, particularly running and complex movement exercises, like taiji chuan (Tai Chi), yoga and dance, all enhance cognitive functioning. In the book, *Spark*, Dr. John Ratey devotes an entire chapter to explaining how movement and physical exercise improve cognitive functioning and attention (2008). One of the points he makes is that there seems to be some extra cognitive benefit derived from physical activities that require you to use your brain in conjunction with complex movements. Based on this research, we know that involving the body in your plan to improve cognitive functioning can be very powerful on many levels. We are, after all, a mind/body; what we do to the body directly influences the mind and vice versa.

In this section, our interest is in finding ways to use the body to assist with the meditative process.

HANDOUT — **STANDING MEDITATION**

In Qigong practices, most of the meditation is done from a standing position. I have found this to be a particularly helpful strategy for those individuals that tend to fall asleep if they sit still for longer than 2 minutes. Because of the way you are standing and the intense attention paid to bodily states, it is also a nice practice for developing attention to detail as well as self-monitoring.

- Stand with your feet shoulder width apart, toes pointing forward

- Adjust the weight distribution on your feet so that you are perfectly balanced, not learning forward or back. Not leaning to either side.

- Sink the energy of the body into the feet. The feet become heavy, grounded and rooted. It is as if you are a tree and there are roots extending from your feet deep into the Earth. The upper part of the body is empty and free to flow in the breeze.

- Keep the knees slightly bent

- Notice the tension in the backs of the legs and allow that to relax as much as possible. Use minimal muscles to hold your body in this position.

- Relax the tailbone, allowing it to point down toward the Earth. It is as if you are just beginning to sit into a chair, keeping the back flat without forcing anything.

- The spine is straight and long. Staying rooted to the Earth, imagine being gently pulled up from the center of the head, as if you are being stretched from the inside.

- Allow the breathing to be slow, long, relaxed and natural in the belly.

- Keep the shoulders dropped. If you are not sure, raise the shoulders up toward the ears and then let them go.

- There is a small gap in the armpits.

- There is a slight bend in the elbows, wrist and every joint of every finger.

- The arms float up in front of the body as if you are hugging a tree. The palms of the hands face the heart, the elbows are down, and the shoulders are dropped.

- The tip of the tongue rests gently on the roof of the mouth

- Relax the muscles of the face and head.

- Put a very slight grin on your face. So slight that someone watching you may not even see it.

- Hold this posture for as long as you can without creating unnecessary tension. Continually checking in with the body, breath and mind. Any time you find tension in the body, see if you can release it just a little bit more. Remind the breath to stay slow, long and natural in the belly. Keep the mind focused on the posture and the breath, if it strays, gently bring it back to task, checking the body and breath and making slight adjustments the entire time and. . .keep the slight grin!

Variation: Utilize the information in the box titled, "Focused Attention in Yoga: Drishti" to focus the gaze during this practice. You might choose as a visual target the fingertips or something in the distance, such as a tree.

HANDOUT — QIGONG
BREATH FOCUS

One strategy to help anchor attention is by adding a simple arm movement to the traditional attention on the breath.

This exercise can be done from either a standing or seated position.

- To begin, allow the hands to rest either at the sides of the body (standing) or with hands on the knees (sitting).

- As you inhale, gently and smoothly raise the arms in front of the body.

- Engage the arms and hands as if these limbs were heavy and did not want to move.

- Imagine the arms being pulled up by the wrists.

- Use as little muscle tension as possible, as if the arms were floating up, perhaps suspended in water.

- Keep the shoulders relaxed (do not raise them).

- Allow the movement to be flowing and soft, matching the quality of the breath.

- Time the arm movements with the breath cycle so that when the inhalation is completed the hands are at shoulder height.

- As you begin the exhalation, allow the arms to float back down, again, as if the movement was led by the wrists.

- Time the movements so that the hands are at the level of the waist at the end of the exhalation.

Variation: Rather than moving the arms in front of the body, raise them on the outside of the body with the inhalation, palms up, as if you are gathering energy around the body. The arms form a circle by moving overhead. The inhalation is completed with the palms of both hands facing the top of the head. On the exhalation, both arms trace down the midline of the body.

HANDOUT — WALKING MEDITATION
BREATH FOCUS

For this practice, you only need about 15 feet of unobstructed room to move. This could be done either inside or outside. If done outside, it is best to find a relatively level area free from rock or tree debris.

- Begin by standing at one end of your path, becoming completely present in your body.

- Sink the energy into the feet, allowing them to feel grounded and rooted.

- As you inhale, slowly and carefully raise one foot.

- As you exhale, place this foot a short distance in front of you.

- With the next inhalation, raise the rear foot.

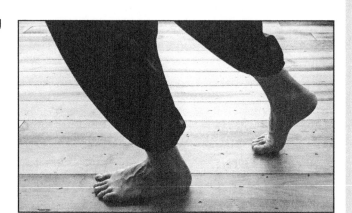

- With the next exhalation, place this foot a short distance in front of you.

- As you reach the end of your path, slowly and methodically, with full attention to your feet and their connection to the Earth, turn around to face the opposite direction.

- Pause at the beginning of your return path.

- Watch your breath for 2-3 cycles.

- Begin the focused attention walking back to the other side.

This practice is designed to be slow. Allow the breathing to be slow, relaxed and balanced-keeping the inhalation and exhalation equal. The goal is not speed. There is no destination. You are simply walking with full attention on the breath and the feet on the ground.

FOCUSED GAZE IN YOGA
DRISHTI

Drishti is the practice of using a focused gaze during asana practice (yoga poses). Essentially, for each pose, there is a point/direction for the visual attention.

Typical places of focus include the middle of the thumb, the forehead (third eye), the palm of the hand or the tips of the toes.

If you are a yoga practitioner and interested in developing your concentration, this would be an important area to explore. If your yoga instructor does not provide this level of instruction or you practice yoga on your own, you can find a natural place to focus the gaze in each pose or read specific descriptions of each pose which is likely to indicate where the gaze should be held.

Websites such as www.yogajournal.com provide detailed instructions for every yoga pose, including the point of attention.

TECHNOLOGY-BASED ASSISTANCE

Thus far, this chapter has outlined the uses of a specific style of meditation to develop increased concentration and focus and to reduce distractibility. The practice is clear, the research is convincing and the brain science makes perfect sense. You have also been shown some helpful tips and strategies to assist in the process. Unfortunately, this knowledge does not make the practice any easier. In fact, this style of meditation might be particularly difficult for someone with attention problems. While we do not want clients to become dependent on specific tools or meditation aids, these can be extremely helpful when attempting to begin a focused attention practice.

RECORDED
GUIDED MEDITATION

Whether done in a live, group meditation or by listening to an audio recording, having someone talk you through an entire meditation can be extremely helpful. Hearing a regular stream of prompts and instructions provides the listener with consistent reminders to keep the mind on the focus of the practice.

As you explore various recorded meditations, be aware that many will include other meditative styles (mindfulness, lovingkindness, etc.). This is not necessarily a bad thing, but something to be aware of. If you are attempting to work specifically with a Concentration practice, make sure you look for descriptions using words such as "focus," and "concentration."

Some free meditations that fall into this category can be found at the NeuroMeditation Institute website: www.NeuroMeditationInstitute.com under the heading "tools."

HANDOUT — MEDITATION AID
INSIGHT TIMER

While many persons with ADHD and similar difficulties may be able to engage in Focus practices as they are described, others will struggle with these practices. While some level of struggle can be good, too much will often lead the person to discontinue the practice. Phone apps such as the Insight Timer offer tools that can be very helpful to the new meditator.

1. **Timer:** At its most basic level, the Insight Timer is exactly what it sounds like. You can set the timer for the length of your meditation and at the end of that time, a meditation bell sounds-signaling the end of the practice. This feature can be helpful in at least two ways. By setting the timer, you can begin to let go of the time watching that often happens with beginning meditators. In addition, this is a great way to track progress as you begin to increase the length of each meditation session.

2. **Tracking:** This app offers a feature similar to fitness apps that allow you to track your practice sessions over time. In this way, you can see how many days and minutes you have been practicing. This can be very rewarding for someone that begins with 3 minutes, advances to 5 minutes and then 10. To have a visual representation of this progress is encouraging.

3. **Interval Bells:** The Insight Timer has a feature that allows you to set a secondary bell to chime at timed intervals throughout the meditation. This additional information can serve as a gentle prompt; an opportunity to examine the focus of attention. If the mind is wandering and the meditator is lost in a fantasy, the chiming of the bell immediately leads you to become aware of the mind's inattention. These interval bells can serve as training wheels assisting the beginning meditator in stabilizing the attention.

4. **Guided Meditations:** This app includes a variety of guided meditations, by different guides for varied lengths of time. Having a voice reminding you of the practice can be very helpful. For many beginning meditators, the mind wanders and may become involved in a prolonged fantasy or memory. This can still occur when using a guided meditation, however, it is likely that the mind will become aware of the voice instructing them which is a call back to the practice.

Heart Rate Variability Biofeedback

Biofeedback is the practice of using some form of external monitoring to increase awareness of an internal physiological process. Most commonly the functions monitored include processes that are outside of conscious awareness, such as skin temperature, sweat gland activity, and heart rate variability. Because our state of consciousness influences our physiology, the ability to "see" and "hear" what is happening in the body during a meditation practice can be extremely helpful. For example, one of the techniques I use frequently involves monitoring heart rate variability.

Because the heart is intimately connected to the lungs and the transportation of oxygen, the heart and respiration patterns are often closely linked. When someone is breathing at a nice, slow, relaxed pace, the inhalation coincides with increases in heart rate and exhalations coincide with decreases in heart rate. This fluctuation of the heart rhythm can be displayed on a computer monitor such that it becomes the point of focus for the meditation/breathing practice. Rather than only focusing on the feeling of the breath moving in and out of the nostrils, you have data about your heart rhythm and breathing pattern being displayed on a computer monitor.

During a biofeedback meditation, you are helping your nervous system attain a state of balance and giving the mind something concrete and external to attend to, moment-to-moment. Rather than simply monitoring, you can also receive feedback about the heart rhythm such that when the pattern is smooth and consistent the client hears a pleasant sound and when the pattern becomes "rough" or inconsistent, they receive a less pleasant tone. Using this as a meditation, you can simply direct the client to watch the heart rate pattern and attempt to make it as smooth and consistent as possible by

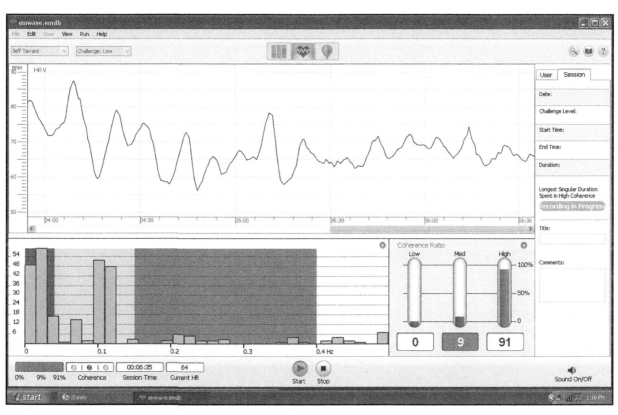

making their breathing smooth and consistent. In essence, they are doing a breath focused meditative practice while using another avenue to develop self-awareness.

As a person engages in this form of practice, the mind inevitably wanders from the breath. As the mind begins worrying or planning or remembering it creates a very mild stress response in the nervous system, which changes the breathing to a more shallow and choppy pattern. The biofeedback software interprets this as being out of balance and provides a deep tone, drawing your attention back to the practice and the fact that your mind has wandered and your breath has become unsteady. It is like meditation training wheels!

The previous screenshot shows a heart rate variability biofeedback screen using em Wave Pro software from the Institute of HeartMath. You can see the fluctuations of the heart rate reflected in the sine wave. On the left-hand portion of the screen, the pattern is larger, smoother and more consistent. As the session continues, the pattern becomes more "choppy" and inconsistent. This pattern is translated into both visual and auditory signals to let the user know how well they can maintain a state of nervous system balance. For more information about HeartMath and heart rate variability biofeedback visit their website at: www.heartmath.org.

EEG-Guided NeuroMeditation

Many beginning meditators complain that they "do not know if they are doing it right." In fact, this may be a reason for discontinuing to practice. They are sitting down every morning, but have no idea if they are entering the "right" state of consciousness. To help clients find the state they are seeking, we can actively monitor their brainwave patterns while they are engaging in specific meditation practices. This allows us the opportunity to actually see if, when and how the client is moving into the desired state. In fact, we can isolate brainwaves in the brain regions of interest and provide a pleasant auditory tone when the brain is doing what we ask, giving the person immediate feedback about their "success" at entering a meditative state.

In the case of a Focus meditation, we can provide a pleasant sound when beta2 or gamma activity increases in the ACC (indicating activity and sustained attention). We can also provide a second tone that signals increases in alpha activity in the DMN (indicating lack of activity and lack of mind wandering). Of course, the ultimate goal would be to keep both sounds going at the same time. A client engaged in this type of neuromeditation training described the process in the following way:

> *"If I focus too much or too narrowly, the feedback stopped, and when both (tones) had been going for a while, I felt very relaxed but still had to maintain some focus/ attention on the tone or breath, otherwise one of the tones would stop. To keep both of them (tones), it was a balance."*

What makes this type of training so powerful is that, as the meditator, you receive immediate feedback (lack of tone) as soon as the mind wanders and becomes distracted. This change in stimulus immediately brings your attention to the fact that you no longer have a single point of attention, allowing you to quickly return to the focus of the meditation.

HANDOUT — MEDITATION AID:
EXTERNAL BREATHING PACERS

External breathing pacers are another tool designed to help focus the attention on the breath. In fact, many biofeedback systems (including HeartMath) include some form of external breath pacer in their software. There are also stand-alone breath pacers that are available for use on a smart phone or computer, making them much more accessible (and affordable). While stand-alone breath pacers do not provide any feedback about your breath or breathing pattern, they do provide another way to focus the mind and breathing.

Try This

1. Go to the website www.doasone.com

2. Click on the tab at the top labeled "rooms"

3. Click on the tab labeled, "cbp" (this stands for custom breath pacer)

4. Choose 6 bpm (breaths per minute)

5. Follow the instructions and use the expanding tear drop form to become your single point of focus for your meditation.

6. If this pace feels too fast, go back and select 7 bpm.

Chapter 3 — BACK FROM THE FUTURE:
Anxiety, Stress and Mindfulness Meditation

WHY ZEBRAS DON'T GET ULCERS

When it is helpful, anxiety can create heightened levels of awareness, arousal and motivation. These qualities can be very useful and adaptive, giving us the energy we need to anticipate and manage problems in our environment. However, for most of us, anxiety has a negative connotation and suggests things like nervousness, worry, fear and apprehension.

While each of these "symptom" words has a distinct flavor, they also have much in common. When we experience any of those feeling states listed above, we are typically anticipating something bad happening in the future. When you worry, what do you worry about? If you are nervous or afraid, what is it in relation to? If you consider this for a moment, you will recognize that in each case your anxiety is built on the expectation of a negative future event. What if my parents become sick? What if my contract isn't renewed? What if my friend is mad at me? What if everyone thinks I'm stupid? In each case, the mind is expecting an aversive situation. We are essentially predicting the future and pre-emptively experiencing the pain, sorrow and disappointment that we believe will happen.

In his book, *Why Zebras Don't Get Ulcers*, Dr. Robert Sapolsky very clearly shows that the very thing that makes us human (our big brain) also creates many of our problems. To address the question posed in the title of the book, zebras (and other mammals) don't get ulcers because they respond to stressors in their environment in a way consistent with their physiological makeup. When a zebra is being chased by a lion, the zebra is fully engaged in a stress response. It physiologically responds to the situation by increasing heart rate, shifting blood flow toward large muscle groups and dilating the pupils in the eyes to focus its vision. The zebra's entire being engages in the fight or flight response and it runs for everything it is worth. If it escapes the prowling lion, the stress response shuts down. When this happens the parasympathetic nervous system kicks in facilitating a process of recovery and rest. The zebra returns to eating grass or whatever zebras do, and the situation is over. This is the way mammals were designed to handle stress.

While humans are certainly mammals, our brains have evolved in such a way that we have become susceptible to self-induced stress. We no longer require anything from the environment to trigger a stress response, we can do this simply sitting by ourselves in a safe and comfortable easy chair and imagining that something could go wrong. With anxiety, fantasy becomes reality. Having a large human brain, we can extend our mind into the future and the past. We can anticipate a plan and develop expectations. In fact, we spend a lot of our time engaging in these cognitive activities. Think about your average day and how much time you spend focusing on what will happen later that day, tomorrow or next week. What will you prepare for dinner? What emails do you need to send? Don't forget to call your mother tonight. We can also reach our minds into the past and remember. The capability to plan and remember obviously brings huge advantages to the process of survival. You can learn from your mistakes, anticipate potential problems and develop plans to minimize future difficulties. The disadvantage is that those memories and predictions very often generate a stress response.

Simply recalling a painful event, whether it occurred last week or 20 years ago can initiate a cascade of physiological changes very similar to those experienced by the zebra running for its life. Simply imagining that something bad might happen will also trigger a stress response. Our bodies respond to our mental meanderings as if they were real. We create a stress response every time we expect problems or anticipate that things will be difficult for us. In essence, our thoughts create stress!

THOUGHTS CREATE STRESS

Humans are meaning-making creatures. We are wired to seek out patterns and connections in our environment to help make sense out of the world. We are constantly involved in this process of meaning making by creating narratives about our life, our "selves" and our surroundings. These stories help us feel like the world is predictable. We believe that understanding the world and how things work will allow us to direct our destiny, giving us a feeling of control. If we can predict all the potential problems that come our way, we will then be able to make the "right" decisions to be safe and comfortable. This process is so automatic and constant that we largely do not even recognize that it is happening. It is the background perception, processing and interpretation of our nervous system. Because this process is so natural and easy we are largely unaware that it is happening every moment. We are unaware that the mind is continuously creating stories to explain the world and our place in it.

Once we begin to recognize the existence of this automated meaning-making machine, we must also recognize that the vast majority of the stories created by our mind are inaccurate or just not true. It is as if the mind is attempting to predict every worst-case scenario by bringing up all the things that could go wrong. "If I don't work constantly I will never be able to retire." "Other drivers are thoughtless and careless." "Other people don't like me." These are the stories we tell ourselves.

The vast majority of the stories created by our minds are works of fiction, but still hold tremendous power. Apparently, our mind does not always recognize if something is True (with a capital T) or just something we made up. In either case, it responds as if it is real. If I believe something is real, so does my brain and my body! We are, after all, a mind-body. The two cannot be separated. If you impact the mind, you naturally impact the body and vice versa.

This idea is explored in great detail in the book, *You Are the Placebo* by Dr. Joe Dispenza. There you will find numerous stories of people who either became ill or healed themselves based simply on their beliefs. The power of belief is so strong it can actually kill. There are numerous stories of healthy people who die because they believe they have a terminal illness. This may be the same mechanism involved in "voodoo deaths," where a person believes they have been cursed. We can see the positive power of belief in the training habits of elite athletes. They understand the power of thought and spend a great deal of time engaged in mental rehearsal and visualization. They are creating a belief about their ability to succeed, to complete their event perfectly. We see Olympic athletes waiting for their turn to compete, making micro movements while they mentally rehearse their routine. We now know that mentally visioning a physical movement activates the same muscle groups and brain regions as actually engaging in the movement.

GARBAGE IN,
GARBAGE OUT

On two occasions, I have been asked, "Pray, Mr. Babbage, if you put into the machine wrong figures, will the right answers come out?" . . . I am not able rightly to apprehend the kind of confusion of ideas that could provoke such a question."

—Charles Babbage, Passages from the Life of a Philosopher

GIGO or Garbage in, Garbage out was originally a phrase used by computer programmers to refer to the impact of running bad data through a logical system, such as a computer. Essentially, if you input bad data, you will get bad results. Of course, there are lots of other applications for this phrase, including what happens when you input "bad data" into the human computer.

When considering that the mind. . .our thoughts, perceptions, and beliefs are essentially programmed by what we are exposed to, it makes sense that we should be very cautious about what kind of inputs we allow into the system.

Everything we are exposed to becomes part of our background, subconscious programming. Everything we watch on television, hear on the radio and observe from our peers and colleagues. All of it plays a role in our perception of the world around us.

If we are interested in cultivating a mind that is relaxed, confident, compassionate and tolerant then it becomes critical that these are the kinds of messages we expose ourselves to.

Visualizing something happening activates the brain in similar ways to the event actually occurring. The brain uses mental rehearsal as a mechanism to lay the groundwork for future movement. Basketball players who spend time everyday imagining themselves making free throws improve their free throw percentage even if they do not spend any extra time physically practicing that skill. Your mind-body adapts to whatever you give it. If you give the mind thoughts and emotions about improving a skill, the body will respond accordingly. If you make up stories about something stressful or dangerous happening, your body will also respond accordingly. So, to say that most of our stress is "in our heads" is very accurate!

It's worth thinking about how this might happen on any given day. A driver cuts you off and you "know" that they did this on purpose. You become angry and respond by "riding their bumper." Your romantic partner does not respond to your repeated texts and you are positive they are ignoring you. You get your feelings hurt and become angry and distant when they do finally get in touch. In both cases, you told yourself a story about what was happening for the other person. In reality, you have no idea what was going on in their lives that may have led to their behavior. It is just as likely that the other driver did not see you and felt really bad for cutting you off. Maybe they were on their way to the hospital to visit a dying relative and were completely distraught and distracted. If that were the story, would you still be angry and driving aggressively or would you suddenly have compassion and empathy for that other driver? Maybe your partner's phone died or they were right in the middle of an important phone call, which is why they could not respond to your texts. Would that change how you felt?

It is not likely that these other stories are true, but it is also not impossible. Your brain, however, automatically fills in all the missing details of any particular situation based on your fears, unmet needs, memories and expectations. Perhaps most shockingly, it does this without your permission and without your even knowing about it. It does this all the time in virtually every situation. Your unconscious thoughts about how unfair and miserable the world is dictate your emotional state and directly influence how you react. In fact, it is safe to say that the vast majority of our processing and mental perceptions are happening outside of our awareness. We generally move through life without understanding why we behave the way we do and without noticing what is happening moment to moment in our daily lives.

THOUGHTS ARE **NOT FACTS**

- Thoughts are passing phenomena. They do not last. They are simply events of the mind.
- Our minds are quick to jump to conclusions out of habit or unawareness.
- Our views of events and ourselves are shaped by prejudices and beliefs, likes and dislikes we have acquired over our lifetime.
- You can learn to manage the power of your thoughts by learning to be more present and to pay attention to the impact your thoughts have.
- By being present you can observe your thoughts without identifying with them.
- It is not necessarily about changing your thoughts, rather changing your relationship to your thoughts.

WORKSHEET — **PRACTICE OBSERVING AND NOTICING**

Mindfulness involves paying attention to what is happening in the moment. Most often when this is discussed, it is in relation to our own thoughts, feelings, bodily sensations, and behaviors. It is also important for us to notice what is happening in our environment. This exercise stretches our observing and noticing muscles.

Wherever you are, make a concerted effort to become curious about your environment and use all your senses:

1. What do you see? What are the shapes? Colors? Textures? Look up. Look Down. Intentionally shift the eyes to areas of the space you wouldn't normally see. Can you simply see without judging?

2. What do you hear? Listen for the obvious sounds and then shift you hearing so you hear the background sounds that you normally filter out. Can you distinguish the "layers" of sound in your environment? Can you simply hear without judging?

3. Continue exploring what you smell and feel and taste in a similar way. Notice the tendency to attach significance to something (I like this, I don't like that).

4. What do you sense? Beyond the 5 senses that you just explored, what else do you feel or notice about the situation. What do your "vibes" tell you?

HANDOUT — **SLOW DOWN!**

Mindfulness, by definition, means paying attention in the present moment. This is very hard to do in a lifestyle moving 180 miles per hour. The speed of life continues to increase and we are inundated with information as well as the expectation that we should always be available by phone, text, or Facebook. In addition, many people use a frantic lifestyle as a distraction so they do not have to experience underlying feelings of sadness, grief, remorse and fear. One of the most powerful and important exercises to begin to shift out of stress mode, is to SLOW DOWN.

Below is a list of ways you can begin to slow down your life. Choose a few of these and make a concerted effort to practice every day.

- Drive slower.

- Put your phone away.

- Take leisurely walks outside.

- Take breaks during the day.

- Take a nap.

- Lie in bed for a few minutes in the morning before getting up.

- Consciously slow your breathing (see RSA breathing exercise at the end of this chapter).

- Pause after finishing a task.

- Spend time alone.

HANDOUT — ACTIVE STORYTELLING

Not only does the mind create stories about ourselves, it also creates stories about other people. This is the basis of judgment. In fact, social psychology research has demonstrated very clearly that we make judgments about other people within moments of meeting them, this is how automatic and unconscious these processes are. We make judgments without even knowing we are doing so. In this exercise, you are encouraged to become more aware of these stories by engaging with them.

1. Find a comfortable public place to hang out where there are likely to be an assortment of people.

   a. Coffee shop
   b. Library
   c. Park
   d. Downtown street corner

2. Pick a random person to observe.

3. As you watch them, make up a story about that person: Who they are, what they are doing, what they are like, how they came to be here right now and what is going to happen next.

   a. Have fun
   b. Be creative
   c. Do this with a friend and share your stories out loud (but not loud enough for anyone else to hear).
   d. If you notice the mind creating negative stories or things that are unpleasant, consciously change the story to make it positive.

4. Pick another person/couple/group and do it again!

You will quickly realize that the point of this exercise is not to sit around judging people, but to recognize that you already do this anyway (just not consciously). This exercise helps you to recognize that your judgments are just stories. Because they are just stories, you can make up anything you want. You do not have to be controlled by the automatic stories of the mind.

AUTOMATIC PILOT

Have you ever had the experience of driving your car to work or around town or maybe on a long trip to another state to visit relatives and realized at some point that you have no memory or awareness of how you got to your destination? Rather than focusing on the task of driving, which actually involves many, many details and sub-tasks, your mind was elsewhere. Perhaps you were thinking about the rest of your day or planning an event, worrying about your children or comparing your experience with a previous trip. You did not notice the traffic lights, the other cars, the way you navigated around the bicyclists. Somehow you did all these things, but with no consciousness! On the one hand that is pretty impressive. On the other hand, it exemplifies how much of our day-to-day lives is conducted on autopilot.

Certainly, there are some benefits to this preset mode of operation. If we had to pay attention to every detail of everything we did, we would not get anything accomplished. It would be extremely inefficient. In fact, our brains automatically filter the vast majority of information that it receives so that you (your conscious mind) only has to tune in to those things that are the most immediately relevant. The bad news is that this process allows us to time travel, spending much of our daily life in the past or the future, missing the beauty and magic of what is happening in the moment.

Fortunately, the majority of these instances take place when you are engaged in "mindless" activities such as taking a shower, cleaning the house, mowing the lawn, working out at the gym or eating a meal. The routinized, "boring" parts of life that we do every day do not require our attention. We can accomplish them with virtually no awareness, as if we were on auto pilot. In fact, in our world of multi-tasking, high efficiency and achievement orientation, we are much more likely to engage in these activities from a state of automatic pilot than from conscious awareness. If you want to think about this using the language of attention, we are constantly distracted. Our attention is not in the present moment. Rather than attending to what is actually happening right now, we fill that time with mental story-telling, we explore fantasies and concerns about what might happen later today, tomorrow or next week. We think that somehow attempting to predict problems will alleviate stress. At the very least, we won't be disappointed if things don't work out the way we wanted. The reality is that the majority of those thoughts that run through our mind are fear-based stories that create an internal environment priming our brain to be stressed and anxious.

This is where mindfulness comes in. Can you become aware of the stories you are telling yourself in any given moment? Can you recognize that your thoughts are not facts? When you are unaware, you act out of habit and the old, tired programming runs the show. When you become aware, you have choice.

EXERCISE — **ONE THING AT A TIME**

Choose a daily activity. Something that you normally do on auto pilot. Examples might include:

- Brushing your teeth

- Taking a shower

- Eating lunch

- Doing the dishes

- Working out at the gym

- Walking the dog

Identify one activity and for the next week, intentionally pay full attention to what is happening in that moment. If you are doing the dishes, just do the dishes. If you are brushing your teeth, just brush your teeth. For those few minutes, there is nothing else to do, there is nowhere to go.

Notice sensory information (what do you see, hear, smell, feel). Notice bodily sensations, emotions and thoughts. Notice how changing your attention changes the experience.

After the first week, choose a different activity. Continue this practice for several weeks and then begin to include this in activities throughout the day.

Not only will this improve your attention, it will also increase your appreciation.

MINDFULNESS WEDGE

When we are operating on auto pilot, we are acting out of habit. This is a state that is largely unconscious. We cruise through our daily lives allowing people and events to happen around us without our full attention. In this state, we end up reacting to our situation from a place that is driven by our subconscious fears and unmet needs, not by what is actually happening in the moment.

No one is immune to acting out of habit. For example, just the other day my life partner was expressing concern about finding a house to buy. We have been renting for the last year and are ready for something more permanent. If we don't find something soon, we will be forced to either renew our lease or find another rental. As she was talking about this situation I became increasingly agitated. I wondered why she was being so negative. Why couldn't she just trust the Universe and accept that things always happen for a reason? She seemed to be focusing on the worst possible scenario, and I was annoyed. As I looked at my reaction a bit more closely it became obvious that I did not want to hear her concerns because it forced me to acknowledge my own anxiety. I am very good at denying my own discomfort and ignoring the negative because I do not want to experience the stress, frustration and fear associated with the idea that we will not find a house in time. My reaction to my partner actually had very little to do with what she was doing or saying and a lot to do with my attempts to avoid my own anxiety.

For most of us, this kind of thing is not unusual. In fact, it is probably typical. We are repeatedly triggered by something in our lives that leads us to behave defensively. Usually, this trigger connects to something from our past or a fear for the future. To avoid this reactivity, it is necessary to interrupt the automatic process. Somehow, we must recognize the process at work and take a time out, allowing ourselves to return to the present; to re-assess or accept what is actually happening. This space between the triggering situation and our reaction is sometimes referred to as a "mindfulness wedge." Imagine that you are inserting a moment of mindfulness just prior to your reaction. This idea has been used in anger management and couples therapy programs for a long time. By interrupting the automatic hurt or anger that we often feel in certain situations, we create an opportunity for something more honest, appropriate and authentic to emerge. By becoming aware of the unconscious processes driving our emotional reactions we create choice and the opportunity to live a more conscious life; a life defined by our intentions rather than our instincts.

EXERCISE — **MINDFULNESS WEDGE**

The basic idea with this exercise is to recognize that you cannot change habits and patterns without first becoming aware of the process. Awareness is necessary for change.

1. Begin to notice common cues that signal you have been triggered. Usually, these are situations in which your reaction to the situation is much stronger than is called for.

2. When you notice that you are beginning to experience symptoms of an overreaction, take a time out

   a. Remove yourself from the situation
   b. Be alone
   c. Take several long, slow breaths

3. Be compassionate toward yourself. Acknowledge that having strong reactions is simply part of being human. You are actively working to understand this better.

4. Ask yourself the following questions:

   a. What emotions are present? (hurt, anger, fear)
   b. What bodily sensations do you notice? (heart racing, muscle tension, headache)
   c. What thoughts emerge? ("I hate this" "I can't stand this," "this is unfair")

EXERCISE — **CHALLENGING THE STORYTELLER**

The mind automatically creates stories about the people and events in our lives. These stories are almost entirely false-works of fiction-based on habits of thinking, fears and childhood imprints. These stories reflect our subconscious programming which very often is in control of our lives. The most basic way to challenge the storyteller is to simply expand on the Mindfulness Wedge exercise.

1. **Observe:** Recognize the story you are telling yourself
   a. Any time you find yourself in a bad mood, upset, or angry about something, pause for a moment and attempt to identify what story you are telling yourself about the situation.
   b. Identify any themes in the story, for example:
      - I am unlovable
      - Life is unfair
      - I don't deserve to feel good
      - People can't be trusted

2. **Question:** Ask yourself some basic questions about your story and the themes.
   a. Is this true?
   b. How do I know this?
   c. Is this an old story? One that I have heard before?

3. **Challenge:** Serve as your own coach and challenge these automatic messages.
   a. Remind yourself that thoughts are not facts
   b. Imagine a new or different interpretation of the situation
   c. Think of an exception to the themes you identified

For a much more sophisticated and elegant approach to this exercise check out the Q Effect (www.theqeffect.com). There you will find resources, programs in your area and information on how to participate in a 21-day self-exploration.

STRESS, ANXIETY AND THE BRAIN

When talking about the brain (and brainwaves), it is important to keep in mind that "one size does not fit all!" What that means is that any particular brainwave pattern cannot be used to diagnostically state with any certainty what is happening for a particular person. Just because two people have similar brain patterns, they may share very little in the way of observable symptoms. Things like temperament, genetics, environmental support, exposure to trauma and diet will all help to determine the specifics of how a particular brain pattern might express itself. At the same time, there are brain patterns that are fairly reliable and consistent among persons with specific mental health concerns.

One such pattern observed in persons experiencing chronic stress and anxiety is an excessive amount of fast brain waves (beta or high beta). This is one of those patterns that makes a great deal of intuitive sense. If there is too much fast activity—more than is needed—this signifies a brain that is overactivated. This can show up as overthinking, cognitive rigidity, worry, fear, agitation and sleep difficulties. An imperfect but perhaps useful analogy relates to caffeine. What happens when you have too much coffee? Most people become anxious, agitated, fidgety and don't sleep well. It is a similar process, but for some, and perhaps for you or a client, it is like this all the time! The nervous system rarely gets a rest. Interestingly, this fast brain wave activity does not consistently show up in the same areas on the surface of the brain. The excess activity may show up in frontal areas, down the midline or in the back of the head. There simply is no reliable way to predict where the excess fast activity may appear. However, when you look just below the cortex, there is an area down the center of the brain that is very often involved in the stress response. This part of the brain is called the cingulate cortex.

The Cingulate Cortex or Cingulate Gyrus is a strip of brain material that connects the cortex with the limbic system. This bridging role is very important as it facilitates communication between the higher functions of the cortex-things like motivation and attention with the functions of the limbic system: emotion processing, learning and memory. When this part of the brain is functioning optimally, we are operating from an integrated place and running efficiently. We are able to effectively process cognitive and emotional inputs, make appropriate decisions and then develop a plan of action. When we are chronically stressed or anxious, this part of the brain becomes overaroused, leading to rigid thinking, stuck emotional states and obsessive or compulsive behaviors. In fact, many experts in the field of neurofeedback have recognized that this part of the brain often seems over active in individuals diagnosed with Obsessive-Compulsive Disorder and Eating Disorders.

When considering the possibility that chronic stress and anxiety may be related to an overheated cingulate, the obvious solution is to cool it down. From a brainwave perspective, we often attempt to create balance in this region by encouraging brainwaves responsible for a more relaxed state. If you remember from Chapter 1, faster brainwaves are associated with activation and concentration while slower brainwaves are associated with deactivation and relaxation. So, if we are interested in quieting down a hot cingulate, the best way to do this might be to increase slow brain waves in that area. Fortunately, one type of meditation practice does just that!

BRAIN REGIONS INVOLVED IN
MINDFULNESS MEDITATION

Anterior Cingulate Cortex (ACC): This region of the brain is involved in several different styles of meditation, but in different ways. The ACC is part of a larger brain structure called the Cingulate Cortex or Cingulate Gyrus. This area of the brain runs right down the midline, connecting the cortex with the limbic system. As such it is involved in many important functions including motivation, attention, switching tasks, emotion processing, learning and memory. When this part of the brain is functioning optimally, we can effectively process cognitive and emotional inputs, make appropriate decisions and then develop a plan of action. When we are chronically stressed or anxious, this part of the brain becomes overaroused, leading to rigid thinking, stuck emotional states and obsessive or compulsive behaviors.

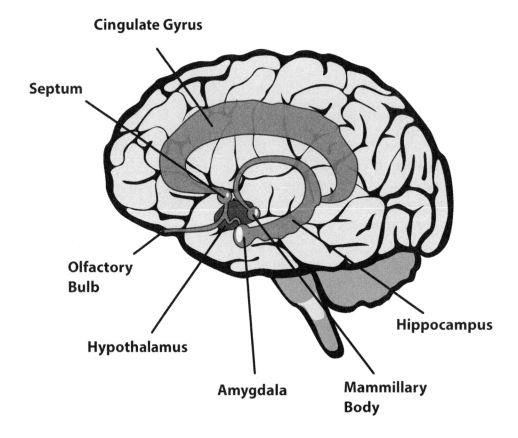

MINDFULNESS MEDITATION

Mindfulness meditation does not involve an explicit attentional focus. Instead, it is characterized by an open presence and a non-judgmental awareness of sensory, cognitive and affective experiences as they arise in the present moment. This type of meditation is often referred to as Open Monitoring meditation (B. R. Cahn & Polich, 2006).

From a Buddhist perspective, the Mindfulness form of meditation practice is called Vipassana or insight practice and can be practiced separately or in conjunction with Focus meditations. While Focus practices are concerned with concentration and attentional stability, in Mindfulness meditation the object of focus is gradually replaced by an effortless sustaining of an open background of awareness without an explicit attentional selection (Lutz, Brefczynski-Lewis, Johnstone, & Davidson, 2008). There is no attachment to a specific object of attention, instead there is a non-reactive monitoring of the content of experience; a moment-to-moment meta-awareness of each thought, bodily sensation and/or feeling state. The handful of research studies examining EEG activity during Mindfulness meditation practices consistently report increases in the amount of slow wave activity (theta) in frontal regions of the brain. This research has also found increases in the shared activity of theta activity in these frontal regions, something referred to as coherence. These findings were consistent among a variety of traditions including Vipassana (B. R. Cahn, Delorme, & Polich, 2010), Zazen (Murata et al., 1994), Sahaja Meditation (Aftanas & Golocheikine, 2001; Baijal & Srinivasan, 2010), and Concentrative Qigong (Pan, Zhang, & Xia, 1994).

MINDFULNESS **BASICS**

There are many styles and traditions of meditation that incorporate Mindfulness techniques. While the specifics of each style may differ somewhat, the general practice typically consists of the following steps:

1. Allow your attention to be relaxed and spacious

2. Notice any bodily sensations, emotions or thoughts that enter your awareness

3. Gently and nonjudgmentally acknowledge whatever arises

4. Let it go and then notice whatever arises in its place

SCRIPT — **MINDFULNESS MEDITATION**

Spend a few moments allowing the body to settle. Feel the weight of the body being supported by your chair or meditation cushion. Can you let go of any unnecessary tension in the body? Scan the body focusing first on the places of obvious tension: the back, shoulders and jaw, then allowing the mind to briefly check in with all of the other parts. Notice the toes, feet, legs, hips, stomach, forearms, hands, lips, ears, eyes and scalp. Let go of any unnecessary tension. Relax.

Allow your attention to also be soft and relaxed. Observe with all your senses. What do you hear? What do you see in your mind's eye? What emotions are present? What bodily sensations do you notice? What thoughts?

Whatever sensation, event or thought seems to have the most salience, simply allow it to be. Acknowledge whatever is present. Without judgment, simply noticing and accepting. Bringing an attitude of openness and curiosity to your experience.

As you notice each new movement of the mind, simply allow it to move on. Let go. The experience is impermanent and can float through your attention like clouds across a blue sky.

Notice the mind's tendency to be attracted to certain thoughts or sensations as well as the tendency to avoid or push away others. Allow every experience to be present and then let it go.

As a reminder, slower brainwaves (like alpha and theta) are associated with a "quieter" mind while faster brainwaves (like beta and high beta) are associated with a "busy" mind. Because theta is a slow brainwave, it seems fitting that it would be related to a deep state of Mindfulness meditation. However, theta in frontal regions of the brain can play more than one role. In addition to suggesting a quieting of mental chatter, theta in frontal midline regions of the brain can also show up when there is a task that requires a certain amount of effort, attention, focus or emotional processing (Aftanas, Lotova, Koshkarov, & Popov, 1998; Aftanas, Varlamov & Pavlov, 2001; Ba ar, Schürmann, & Sakowitz, 2001; Dietl et al., 1999; Dietl, Dirlich, Vogl, Lechner, & Strian, 1999). This special case of theta occurring when the mind is active and focused only occurs in frontal midline areas (the anterior cingulate cortex) and is referred to as the frontal midline theta rhythm or FM theta (Aftanas & Golocheikine, 2001). If FM theta is related to attention, focus and emotional processing, doesn't it make sense that it would appear during a Mindfulness meditation? During a Mindfulness meditation practice you are orienting to whatever is most present in your experience in that moment (body sensations, thoughts, feeling states) and attending to that experience without judgment or attachment. You are holding the attention and focus in a very specific way for a very specific purpose and noticing whatever arises. You are observing "the self."

A study of the Sahaja Yoga meditation tradition offers supportive evidence that theta is specifically associated with a detached awareness of moment-to-moment experiences. This study, which examined a "thoughtless awareness" form of meditation discovered that long term meditators showed different theta activation patterns than short term meditators. Specifically, long term meditators showed increased levels of both general and FM theta power in the brain. This means that experienced meditators in this tradition were both relaxed with a quiet mind (general theta) and utilizing a focused attention with positive emotional experience (FM theta) at the same time. (Aftanas & Golocheikine, 2001, p. 59). Short-term meditators did not show the same type of theta increases. The authors suggested that the newer meditators may not have shown the same brainwave patterns because they were trying too hard to attain a specific meditative state. This study and others like it suggests that the ability to observe the self in a more detached manner leads to increased slow activity in frontal regions while anxiety and frustration are linked to a lack of slow activity in these frontal regions. Stated another way, stress and anxiety increase activation in frontal midline regions, while a relaxed, inclusive attention decreases activation in frontal midline regions.

Notice also that the remedy for an excessive focus on the future is to shift to a present focus. What is happening right now? By understanding the way our attention and thought patterns influence the brain, it becomes clear that changing your mind changes your brain.

When we operate on automatic pilot and allow our subconscious programming to run the show, we give away our control and allow the system to spiral into an unnecessary stress and anxiety response. Simply by learning to pay attention in a different way, we can interrupt this process, quieting the nervous system and giving our poor worried mind a respite.

MINDFULNESS MEDITATION TIP #1
BEGIN WITH THE BREATH

Many meditators will attempt to sit down for their practice and immediately launch into a mindfulness practice. While this is certainly not wrong, it can be challenging. This is often an abrupt transition and the mind is racing so quickly between different thoughts, feelings and perceptions that it can be somewhat overwhelming.

It is generally helpful to take a few minutes at the beginning of a Mindfulness practice to settle the mind and ground the body.

Start your practice by tuning in to the weight of the body on the cushion (or chair). Feel the body being supported. You might specifically tune in to the bottoms of the feet, the palms of the hands and the back to feel more grounded and settled.

Focus on the breath, allowing it to be smooth, rhythmic, fluid and natural. Watch the breath and allow this to be your point of focus for a few minutes. This practice will help settle the mind and slow the onslaught of mental movements.

Once the mind feels somewhat settled and the body feels relaxed and alert, then you can gently shift your attention toward noticing any thoughts, feelings or sensations that arise.

MINDFULNESS MEDITATION TIP #2
ATTITUDE OF CURIOSITY

One of the most challenging aspects of Mindfulness Meditation relates to the tendency of the mind to constantly judge. Think about it, every time you decide you like or don't like something, you have made a judgment. When this happens, the mind is no longer open to what is actually happening. It is now involved in creating a story.

During Mindfulness Meditation practices, we are watching the events of the mind as they move through. We are also attempting to do this in a non-judgmental way. Can you simply recognize what the mind is doing without trying to stop it or getting frustrated or feeling that you are somehow doing it wrong?

A powerful approach to help with the judging mind is to enter meditation with an attitude of curiosity. Can you watch the mind and wonder at its process rather than attempting to control or berate it? When observing the mind and thoughts, it is often helpful to say to yourself, "that's interesting." Be curious. Remember that this process is not necessarily about changing the mind as much as it is about understanding how the mind works. You are a scientist studying the mind. If you can bring this attitude to your practice, you will find that you are less judgmental toward yourself, but also that it is possible to enjoy and laugh at the games the mind plays.

MINDFULNESS TIP #3
LABELING YOUR OBSERVATIONS

It is sometimes helpful to provide a label for the experiences that arise during a Mindfulness practice. For example, if you notice yourself thinking about what you will be doing later that day, you can simply identify this process by saying to yourself, "planning" and then letting it go. Some common labels might also include the following:

- Remembering
- Judging
- Avoiding

- Grasping
- Worrying
- Craving

You may find that the mind has certain behaviors that it engages in consistently or repetitively. You may label the mind's activity as "planning," let that go and find that the mind immediately returns to planning. When this happens, acknowledge the mind's activity, label it as "planning" and let it go again.

If you notice that you begin to have negative thoughts about yourself because of this repetitious mind behavior, simply note that as "judging" and let it go as well.

While all forms of meditation may be beneficial in the management of anxiety symptoms, Mindfulness practices seem to be particularly helpful for the management of anxiety symptoms. Several key research studies provide information that clearly demonstrates the link between brainwaves, anxiety, stress, and Mindfulness.

1) Persons demonstrating greater theta activity tend to report less anxiety (Inanaga, 1998).

2) Mindfulness forms of meditation increase theta activity (Aftanas & Golocheikine, 2001).

3) Increases in frontal theta during meditation have been associated with decreases in both short- and long-term anxiety levels (Shapiro, Jr., 2008; M. West, 1987).

4) A comparison study, examining the EEG signatures of Focus practice versus a Mindfulness meditation found that the Mindfulness practice resulted in higher levels of frontal theta (Dunn et al., 1999).

So, the take home message is this: If you want to improve concentration, do a Focus meditation. If you want to reduce anxiety, do a Mindfulness meditation.

MINDFULNESS
NEUROMEDITATION

Using brainwave feedback to provide a reward signal for increases in frontal theta activation, one of my EEG biofeedback neuromeditation clients described the experience like this:

"This protocol, or at least the way I was approaching the session led to a very mellow, pleasant state of mind. Very calming, slow and relaxed. I just let go of any thoughts and don't try to force anything to happen or to not happen. I seemed to receive the reward when I was a little bit more focused rather than so easygoing as my typical meditation is, or as I would like it to be. I came out of this session not wanting it to end nor wanting to speak or verbalize my experience."

A session review graph, after a period to allow for adjustment to the protocol, clearly shows a gradual increase in FM theta at ACC.

ACC Theta and Precuneus Alpha during a Mindfulness NeuroMeditation session.

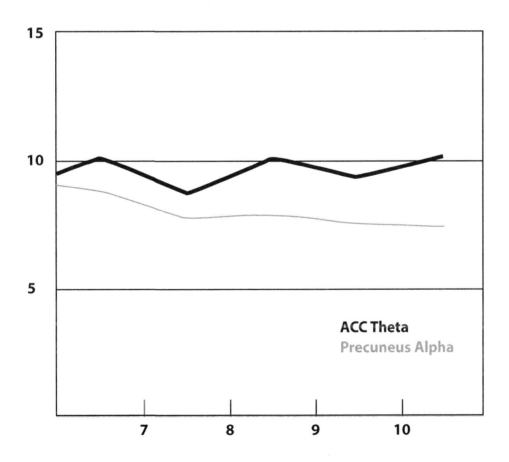

SUPPLEMENTAL STRATEGIES

Movement-based Practices

Practices such as Qigong, Taiji Chuan (Tai Chi), Yoga, Feldenkrais or the Alexander Technique are all considered mindful movement practices. Although quite different in their particular approach and tradition, each of them incorporates present awareness, mindful movement, breathing and a deep state of relaxation (Payne & Crane-Godreau, 2013). A review of the literature related to these types of practices found an overall positive effect on a wide range of mental and physical measures including: depression, anxiety, cognitive ability, inflammation, immune function, arthritis, supportive cancer care, cardiac and pulmonary health, balance, aerobic capacity, strength, bone density, fibromyalgia, and diabetes (Payne & Crane-Godreau, 2013).

It is important to help clients recognize that any of these activities can also be done mindlessly. It is very common, for example, for people to take a yoga or tai chi class for the physical exercise and/or the sense of community. There is certainly nothing wrong with those motivations and I suspect that persons attending class for those reasons find improvements in their physical coordination, balance and social network. However, it also seems likely that you will see additional benefit by engaging in these activities with a mindful attitude; paying close attention to everything that is happening moment to moment. In a yoga class this might mean observing what it feels like for the body to stretch, noticing where your limits are, recognizing pleasure and discomfort, noticing the mind's tendency to compare yourself to other students, recognizing the mind wanting to impress the instructor, recognizing feelings of jealousy of the clothes or gear other students may have. All of these awarenesses might be part of engaging in a yoga class mindfully.

In the same way that someone might attend to yoga or tai chi mindfully or mindlessly, it is also possible to use movement-based practices for a variety of NeuroMeditation styles, depending on one's motivation and intention. If a client were practicing Qigong as a Mindfulness Meditation, they might engage in the repetitive movements attempting to notice whatever is the most present at that time. They might notice the weight of the feet on the Earth, tension in the low back, and the fluidity of the arms moving through space. They might also notice the slowing and quickening of the breath, how the mind worries about doing something correctly or that the instructor will notice their lack of practice. Whatever thought or feeling or bodily sensation is the most present is acknowledged and then allowed to move past. On the other hand, if you wanted clients to use a Tai Chi practice as a Focus meditation, you might instruct them to choose a specific target to hold attention with each repetition of the form. They might choose to focus on the smoothness of each movement or staying rooted throughout the form or they might focus on maintaining a slow, relaxed and natural style of breathing. In this way, they move through the form as the mind remains focused on a single aspect of the practice.

RSA Breathing

In the last chapter, we discussed the role of breathing in meditation primarily as a tool for concentration, a place to focus the mind. In this chapter, we deepen the topic by exploring ways that specific breathing strategies can be used to decrease anxiety and significantly impact the stress regions of the brain.

HANDOUT — **BELLY BREATHING**

Breathing "from the belly" is important to shift out of a stress response. When we are stressed, breathing becomes more shallow, higher in the chest and rapid. When we are relaxed, it tends to lengthen, soften and shift to the belly. By changing breathing patterns, you are signaling to your nervous system that you are no longer in a stress response. It is very difficult for your body/mind to breathe naturally AND maintain a stress response at the same time. It must choose one or the other and you can use this knowledge to actively shift out of a chronic stress response. Belly breathing also allows the lungs to fill more fully, allowing the body and brain to take in more oxygen.

Under the lungs is a sheet of muscle called the diaphragm. This muscle pulls down when we breathe in allowing the lungs to fill with air. The diaphragm releases on the exhale, allowing the lungs to collapse and empty. When we breathe in and the diaphragm pulls down the contents of our guts need to move out of the way. The easiest way for this to happen is for the belly to expand. When this happens, the diaphragm has more range of movement and the lungs can fully expand.

Try this: Suck in your belly as if you were going to the beach and had to wear a bikini or speedo. Hold your gut in and simultaneously try to take a deep breath. It doesn't work! The belly must be relaxed and soft-free to expand and contract in order to fill the lungs.

Belly Breathing Tips:

- Place one hand on your chest and one on the belly. Initially, just notice which hand moves more when you breathe. If the top hand moves more or if the movement between hands is about equal, gently shift the breathing so that the belly expands during inhalation and contracts during exhalation. With a little practice, most people can achieve this fairly easily. By using your hand as a biofeedback tool, you are gaining direct information about the behavior of your breathing.

- Make sure your posture is open as you focus on your breathing. If your body is collapsed forward or you are sitting in an uncomfortable chair, it is likely that the body mechanics required for belly breathing will be difficult or impossible.

- Loosen your clothing. Try not to wear restrictive clothing or if you are practicing your breathing somewhere private, unbutton the top button of your pants and loosen your belt

- Try not to force the breath. See if you can relax into the process. Allow the breathing to be natural and relaxed. Notice any tendency to control or force the breath. Notice that simply relaxing will make the transition much easier.

HANDOUT — **RSA BREATHING**

- Breathe from the belly

- In the beginning, don't worry about the pace too much, focus on the qualities of the breathing. Allow the breath to become smooth, relaxed, gentle, long and natural.

- Don't force it. Tuning in to the concept of natural breathing is the most important step in this process.

- Time your breathing to determine what pace helps you feel somewhat relaxed and natural. You can do this by simply using a clock with a second hand or a stopwatch.

- Allow the inbreath and outbreath to be the same amount of time (ex: 4 seconds in, 4 seconds out)

- Do not try to take in or breathe out more air. A common mistake that people make when beginning to work with the breath involves attempting to increase the length of the breath by either breathing in or breathing out more air. The lungs can only hold so much. Attempts to inhale or exhale more air than the lungs can hold will create more stress. This is why there is a strong emphasis on allowing the breathing to feel natural. The trick is to slow the rate of breathing without changing the overall amount of air used. Imagine that you are breathing through a straw. You can only inhale or exhale a small amount of air at a time. It is as if the airflow was restricted. You can also imagine that your lungs are like a balloon filled with air and you are holding the opening between your fingers. You control how much air comes out at any given moment. Controlling the flow of air is the best way to slow the breathing without creating discomfort or a hyperventilation response.

- If you ever begin to feel light headed or uncomfortable, stop the exercise and assess what you might be doing to influence that reaction. It might be that you are taking too deep or full of a breath when a normal-sized breath would suffice. Return to natural, relaxed breathing.

- Use a breath pacer to help you shift your breathing to 6 breaths per minute. If this is uncomfortable, make it a little faster (ex: 7 breaths per minute)

- Take your time and be patient with yourself.

RSA stands for Respiratory Sinus Arrhythmia. When explaining this, I often joke that it sounds like something you would not want to hear in the doctor's office. "I'm sorry Jeff, but you have respiratory sinus arrhythmia." Despite the very medical sounding name, RSA is just a technical way of describing a pattern of breathing in which your heart rate variability and your breath are synchronized. When you are breathing at your resonant frequency, your heart rate increases as you inhale and decreases as you exhale. Your bodily systems are synchronized and all sorts of interesting, magical things begin to happen. When you breathe at your RSA for 10-15 minutes, stress hormones (cortisol) decrease and DHEA (restoration) hormones increase (McCraty et al., 1998). Breathing at your RSA also quiets down brain regions involved in the stress response. So, when you breathe at your RSA you are not just changing your breathing pattern or your heart, you are changing your entire system. What an incredibly powerful and simple strategy! No wonder ancient practices like yoga and qigong include breathing exercises. Your breathing changes your state of consciousness.

My appreciation for this relatively simple strategy for anxiety reduction was enhanced after reading a 2010 study by Sherlin, Muench and Wyckoff. These researchers took a group of subjects with high levels of anxiety, hooked them up to an EEG machine and then recorded their brainwave activity during a stressful task and then after engaging in RSA breathing for 15 minutes. When the data were analyzed they found significant increases in alpha brain waves in the cingulate gyrus and significant decreases in beta waves in posterior regions of the brain. They also found that the better someone did on the RSA breathing, the more significant the response that was observed. The researchers concluded: "RSA training may decrease arousal by promoting an increase of alpha

EXTERNAL **BREATHING PACERS**

In Chapter 2 you were introduced to the concept of breathing pacers as a tool to help with a concentration, Focus form of practice. For a Focus practice, the pace of the breath is less important than having an external cue to keep the mind on track.

With a Mindfulness practice, designed to reduce anxiety, the pace of the breathing may be important. For most people, their RSA will be around 6 breaths per minute. Without a great deal of practice, it is very difficult to breathe at this rate without some form of feedback or method to pace your breathing.

While each specific breath pacer differs in appearance and settings options, they all offer animations and/or sound patterns prompting you to inhale and exhale at a specified rate. You can choose the breathing rate on these programs, in some cases with great specificity. For example, many techniques focus on breathing at the rate of 6 breaths per minute (bpm) to quiet the nervous system. You can set the pacer for 6 bpm, which will then prompt you to inhale or exhale every 5 seconds (10 second breathing cycle equals 6 breathing cycles in 1 minute). Some programs allow you to specify the length of time for each component of the breath cycle (inhalation, pause, exhalation, pause). You can find these applications on your smartphone by typing "breath pacer" into your App store or Google Play search bar. Some of the more well-known pacers include: My Calm Beat and Do As One.

band frequencies and decrease in beta frequencies overall and in areas critical to the regulation of stress." So, while this training seems to impact alpha rather than theta, it appears to have a very similar outcome, quieting the anterior cingulate, reducing beta and reducing the stress response.

Learning to breathe at your resonant frequency is often a step-wise process. First, it is important to learn to relax the breathing and allow it to occur naturally. This type of breathing is often called "belly breathing" or "diaphragmatic breathing." Once this type of breathing has been accomplished, helping the breath to become quiet, slow, relaxed and gentle, the next step is establishing the pace of breathing. When you are able to take the "belly breathing" technique and apply it at a slow, paced rate (usually 6 breath cycles per minute), then it becomes RSA breathing.

Finding your precise RSA is a little bit of an individual process and requires some physiological monitoring equipment, typically a pneumograph (breathing monitor) and something to measure heart rate variability. However, the vast majority of people have their RSA right around 6 breaths per minute. Some people are a little slower, some a little faster, but almost everyone is between 5 and 7 breaths per minute. This is pretty slow, especially considering that the average breathing rate for adults is somewhere between 12 and 15 breaths per minute. To breathe at 6 breaths per minute, you would complete one breath cycle (inhalation and exhalation) every 10 seconds; 5 seconds in, 5 seconds out. For most people, shifting from 12-15 breaths per minute to 6 is not a terribly smooth transition. It is often best to begin lengthening the breath in a comfortable and gradual way.

ESSENTIAL OILS TO
DECREASE ANXIETY

In Chapter 2, we explored ways that essential oils may impact nervous system functioning and how specific oils may have benefit for attention and focus. Not surprisingly, other oils have impacts that make them ideal candidates for stress and anxiety management.

Rosemary

Rosemary has been found to decrease frontal alpha and beta, lower anxiety scores and result in subjects feeling more relaxed and alert (Diego, et al., 1998).

Linalool

Linalool is a component of essential oils commonly found in Ylang Ylang, Lavender, Frankincense, Myrrh, Lemongrass and others. Research with Linalool has shown it to have anti-anxiety effects as well as the ability to reduce aggression and improve sleep (Guzman-Gutierrez, et al., 2015; Kang & Seol, 2015).

In a single subject case study, this author measured brainwave activity before and immediately after the volunteer placed 2 drops of Frankincense oil on their tongue. The brain images below represent the percent change of alpha and beta activity. Alpha brainwaves increased by up to 12% in parietal and occipital regions (areas of darkest coloration), while fast activity (beta) decreased by up to 13% in a variety of brain regions (areas of darkest coloration).

The simultaneous increase of slow activity (alpha) and decrease of fast activity (beta) suggests a significant quieting of mental activity.

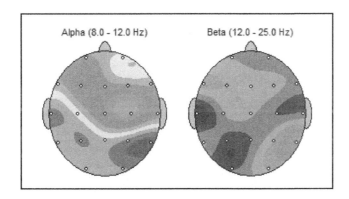

Mandalynth

A Mandalynth is a Celtic art mandala that you trace like a labyrinth. The idea is to simply trace the design with a stylus, capped pen, coffee stir, or anything that points (like your finger). While there are certainly some similarities with coloring, there are also some differences. With the mandalynth, there is no beginning or end. You cannot make any mistakes and there are no decisions to make. Tracing in this way isolates hand-to-eye coordination and tends to have a very quieting effect on the brain.

When I was first introduced to this tool, I was skeptical of the claims that this simple tool could have strong and nearly immediate impacts on the activation patterns of the brain—so I studied it.

With a series of subjects, all experiencing moderate to high levels of anxiety, I analyzed their brainwave activity before and while tracing a mandalynth for 3 minutes. While there are certainly individual differences in response patterns, the overall trend was very clearly in a direction of quieting the brain and the subject feeling an almost immediate decrease in their state anxiety. Some subjects experienced dramatic changes.

Below is Qeeg data from a successful professional woman that experiences very high levels of worry and what might be considered "overthinking." This is someone who is constantly judging and analyzing. The colors for each band (delta, theta, alpha, etc.) represent how much power this person has in relation to a normative database. Pure white would indicate that the amount of activity is about average. As the tones become darker, there is significantly more activity compared to average. As can clearly be seen, this person has an excessive amount of activity in virtually every band. The beta band shows excess activity nearly everywhere.

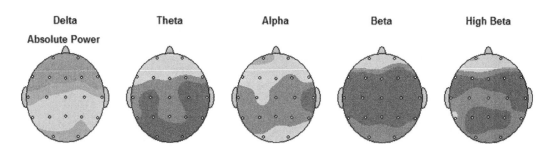

I asked this subject to trace a medium mandalynth with her dominant hand for 3 minutes while I continued to record brainwave data. This is what happened:

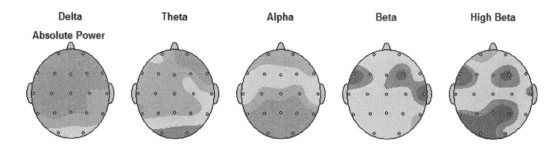

EXERCISE — TRACE THE
MANDALYNTH

Choose a tracing tool. This could simply be your finger (use your middle finger), a stylus or a pen with a cap.

Exercise 1

- Start anywhere on the blue twisting curves of the design and simply begin tracing with your dominant hand.
- Do not worry about staying in the lines. If you lose your place, just continue wherever you are.
- Allow the movements to be flowing, easy and smooth.
- Do this for 3 minutes and notice how you feel.
- Switch hands and repeat.

Exercise 2

- Begin at the tip of any of the three loops in the center of the design using your dominant hand
- Follow the loops from tip to tip, counting in sequence each time you reach another point
  - Counting should move 1-2-3.
  - The third tip returns you to the starting point.
  - Return your counting to 1 and repeat the cycle.
- Allow the counting and the tracing to be easy, smooth and rhythmic.
- Continue for 3 minutes. Notice how you feel.
- Switch hands and repeat.

The Simple Celtic Trinity Knot Mandalynth by Ravensdaughter

There are many different styles of Mandalynths available, some in an open weave, others medium and still others tight. Different people have different preferences, although it has been reported that most people experiencing stress and anxiety prefer an open design (similar to that displayed above). Persons with ADHD and PTSD tend to prefer a medium weave and persons with an autism spectrum disorder prefer the tight designs.

You can download a mobile app for an iPad that provides one sample design of each type. Simply type "Celtic Mandalynth" in your app search.

You can see that the slower brainwave frequencies (delta, theta, alpha) almost completely normalized, while the beta and high beta decreased substantially. Subjectively, this subject reported feeling calmer and having less internal chatter during this experience which is reflected in the brainwave patterns.

In all my years of measuring brainwaves, I have never seen anything change brain patterns that quickly and dramatically. Of course, the obvious question is, "will this last?" The answer is "we don't know." It is possible that with enough practice this new, more relaxed pattern in the brain would become more stable. However, we are generally not looking at this intervention as a complete treatment strategy, but rather as a tool to disrupt an overactivated brain and allow the opportunity for something different to happen. This tool essentially creates a space. It can be used when someone is actively engaged in an anxiety/panic attack, is feeling agitated or hypersensitive or simply as a device to maintain a calm presence. We have placed several of these in our waiting area for clients to work with while waiting for their next appointment with positive results.

MINDFULNESS IN NATURE

Research has clearly demonstrated that spending time in nature has a range of positive benefits for both physical and mental health. In fact, one study with over 11,000 subjects, reported in the book *Your Brain on Nature*, showed that people living further away from green spaces were much more likely to report high stress and had lower scores on a variety of measures including general health, vitality, mental health and physical pain. When comparing subjects that lived near greenspace versus those with little access, it was found that the low access group had a 25% greater risk for depression and a 30% greater risk for anxiety disorders (reported in Selhub & Logan, 2012).

Research using an fMRI scanner found that subjects viewing urban scenery had increased activation in the amygdala and the anterior temporal pole. The amygdala is well-known for its role in the stress response. When it becomes overactivated, the brain becomes overly focused on the negative and "looks" for problems in the environment. On the other hand, when subjects viewed nature scenes, the anterior cingulate and insula became active which is a pattern known to be related to positive emotional states including empathy (reported in Selhub & Logan, 2012).

What this and other research tells us is that we are designed to be in nature. Access to nature and views of nature calm our systems and help us to feel grounded, balanced and quiet. In this way, it should be obvious that spending more time in nature could be a powerful way to shift out of the stress response. Interestingly, it appears that simply viewing nature such as green plants and vistas helps reduce stress and enhance positive emotional states (Berto, 2014; Wells & Evans, 2003). Imagine the positive potential of combining time in nature or views of nature with mindfulness. Doesn't it make sense that this combination would work together, synergistically to reduce stress and anxiety? For those that do not have access to nature because of physical health, location or mobility, it can be very helpful to utilize virtual reality nature based scenes to facilitate this state of mindful awareness.

EXERCISE — OPENING OUR SENSES
MINDFULNESS IN NATURE

Nature is an easy and important avenue to shifting consciousness. You can take advantage of this benefit by simply doing your meditation or qigong or yoga practice outdoors. You can also engage nature in your meditation. Try this:

Find a spot in nature where you can sit comfortably for 15-30 minutes. You may also find a spot that is indoors with a view of nature or use an immersive nature scene in virtual reality. Whatever the location, it is important that you are comfortable.

Spend a few moments allowing the body to settle. Release areas of tension in the body.

Check in with your breathing and invite it to be slow, easy, relaxed and natural.

Now, tune in to your environment. Without actively scanning, allow the sensory experience of the environment to wash over you.

- Notice what the eyes attend to.
- Notice what the ears attend to.
- Notice what the skin perceives.
- Notice what the nose attends to.

Notice how the sights, sounds, and tactile sensations impact your thoughts, feelings and body.

As much as possible do not seek with the senses, simply "be with" whatever is present.

YOUR BRAIN ON VR: THE IMPACT OF **VIRTUAL REALITY MEDITATION** ON **BRAINWAVE ACTIVITY**

There is ample evidence that Virtual Reality experiences of nature can lead people to have physiological responses consistent with the actual natural environment. However, no one has yet examined the impact of VR meditations on the brainwave activity of people using this technology.

For this pilot study, we obtained a baseline measurement of brainwave activity using a 19 channel EEG system. The volunteer then participated in a 4-minute mindfulness in nature experience after which we measured the brainwaves one more time.

Overall, the results showed a significant quieting of the brain after experiencing the brief VR nature meditation, measured by decreases in fast activity (gamma) and increases in slow activity (theta and alpha). This, by itself, was impressive given the relatively brief exposure to the meditation. Perhaps more importantly, an analysis of specific brain regions impacted by the VR meditation showed that areas of the brain involved in the stress response were some of the most significantly impacted. Below are 3D brain images showing changes in the brain after the VR meditation.

The first picture is looking at fast brainwave activity (gamma) in the anterior cingulate. The darker tones indicate that gamma activity decreased significantly during the meditation. This is important because this part of the brain often becomes overactivated during stress and anxiety or when we become fixated on thoughts, feelings or behaviors. By helping this area to relax, the brain is shifting into a more relaxed, peaceful state.

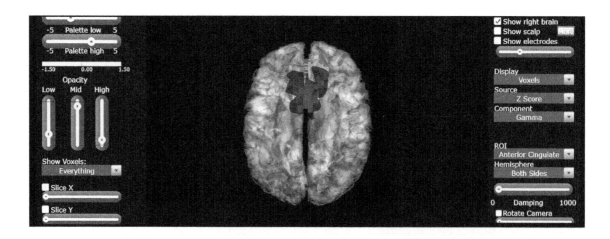

In the next image, we switch from examining fast brainwaves to looking at slow brainwaves. In particular, we are looking at alpha activity in the Precuneus. This part of the brain is the hub of the brain's Default Mode Network (DMN). When the DMN is quieter, as seen here, this suggests that the person is not thinking about themselves (or their worries) as much, which is exactly what we would hope to see during this experience.

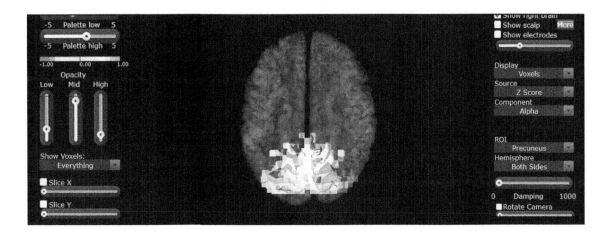

These results provide preliminary evidence that this type of technology can have a nearly immediate impact on the stress response.

See Appendix 2 at the back of the book for information on how to bring Virtual Reality into your practice.

Chapter 4 — THE DEPRESSED BRAIN:
Strategies to Shift Perspective

THE DEPRESSED BRAIN

While there are a variety of brainwave patterns that may "show up" in relation to depressed symptoms, one pattern that has been studied extensively relates to asymmetrical activation patterns in the frontal lobes of the brain. When we compare the left and right frontal lobes of the brain, we consistently find that persons with more activation on the left tend to be more optimistic, flexible thinkers and tend to move toward difficulties in an effort to solve them. Persons with more activation on the right tend to do just the opposite. They are more pessimistic, tend to see the potential problems in a situation and move away from difficulties. Not surprisingly, these trends have been shown to be related to both state and trait mood patterns. For example, a study by Nusslock and colleagues (2007) examined the frontal EEG asymmetry of 59 women with childhood-onset depression and 72 women with no history of depression. Their findings clearly showed that the women with a history of depression had decreased left frontal activity compared to the control group. The investigators also found that subjects that were currently depressed had lower relative left frontal activity than previously depressed persons whose symptoms were currently in remission.

FRONTAL ASYMMETRY AND BRAINWAVES

When we are talking about activation patterns in relation to brainwaves, we can generally understand that fast brain waves (beta) are associated with activation whereas slow waves (alpha) are associated with inactivation. With this understanding in mind, in a healthy, "happy" brain, we expect to see more beta and less alpha on the left side in relation to the right. This is important to understand as most of the research in this area examines alpha asymmetry in frontal regions as a marker of depression. Because the depressed brain tends to have less activation on the left, increases in alpha on this side can be used as a marker for potential mood related issues.

In the world of neurofeedback, we have known about these patterns for many years and developed brain training protocols to shift this balance in depressed individuals toward more left activation. In fact, this is the first thing I look for when someone with depression comes to my office for neurofeedback training-is there a frontal alpha asymmetry? Neurofeedback research dating back to the late 1990's demonstrated that training the brain toward left activation can have significant benefits.

ALPHA
ASYMMETRY

When alpha activity is significantly higher on the left than the right, this can sometimes be a marker for mood related concerns including depression.

Below is a 3D brain image of a depressed client. This EEG analysis software allows us to visualize the amount of brainwave activity in the regions specified. In this case, we are examining alpha activity in the frontal lobes and you can see that the left side is brighter than the right side (dark grey), indicating that there is more alpha on the left.

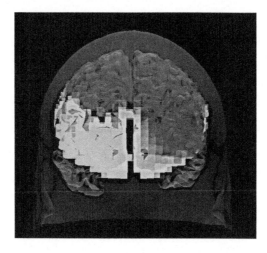

3D sLORETA brain imaging using BrainAvatar software from BrainMaster Technologies.

Baehr and colleagues used an alpha asymmetry protocol in two different sets of case studies to successfully treat depression in patients also being treated with psychotherapy (Baehr & Baehr, 1997; Baehr, et al., 1999). Other research has taken the same idea, but applied it by rewarding left frontal beta activity while inhibiting alpha and theta activity (Hammond, 2000 & 2005).

At this point, we have established that many individuals experiencing depressed symptoms will show decreased activation in left frontal areas in relation to the right. We have also seen that neurofeedback training designed to encourage left frontal activation can be an effective treatment for depression.

If left frontal activation is associated with more positive affect and reduced symptoms of depression, it seems reasonable to consider that specific meditative practices might have a similar impact. Because certain forms of meditation intentionally invoke positive emotional states, such as compassion or gratitude, these practices may directly impact frontal asymmetry and serve as an additional non-medication approach to working with depressive symptoms.

OPEN HEART MEDITATIONS

In Open Heart forms of meditation, the practitioner is attempting to generate specific feelings of love, compassion or peace and then send or offer these feelings to other people, regions of the world or "all sentient beings." During an Open Heart meditation, you might shift the target of your attention throughout the practice. For example, you might begin by sending these feelings to a friend and then shift to a co-worker and then shift again to someone you don't particularly care for. With their emphasis on establishing positive affect and empathy toward others, Open Heart practices may be ideally suited as a treatment intervention for depression, anger, hostility, or mental health concerns that involve a lack of empathy (e.g., personality disorders).

OPEN HEART
BASICS

There are many ways to practice Open Heart meditation based on a variety of traditions. In the literature, these forms of meditation may be referred to as lovingkindness, compassion, or metta.

The general formula for an Open Heart practice looks something like this:

1. Focus the attention on a specific person, issue or regions of the world

2. Intentionally generate feelings of love, compassion, peace, gratitude or forgiveness

3. Send these feelings toward the target of the meditation

4. Shift to another target and repeat the process

Research has demonstrated that long-term Open Heart meditators tend to be happier, less anxious and report stronger coping self-efficacy than novice meditators (Tarrant, 2015). Importantly, other research suggests that even a relatively short training period of Open Heart forms of practice can result in clinically significant results. For example, Carson et al., (2005) reported improvements in the experience of pain after 8, 1 hour sessions. Other research has shown that 12 weekly 2-hour sessions were effective in reducing anxiety, anger and mood difficulties (Gilbert & Proctor, 2006). Another study found that even a single 7-minute Open Heart meditation can produce improvements in positive feelings toward self and others (Hurcherson et al., 2008). Not only do these practices appear to make a significant difference in psychological and emotional states, they also impact areas of the brain associated with emotional processing, empathy and positive feeling (Hoffmann, et al., 2011).

SCRIPT — **LOVINGKINDNESS/ COMPASSION MEDITATION**

Begin by adopting a posture that feels open and receptive. If you will not become excessively drowsy, you might lie down during this meditation. If you are sitting, make sure the chest is open. Allow the hands to rest on the knees, palms up or place the hands over the heart center.

Spend a few moments settling into the body, experiencing the wholeness of the body.

Allow the breath to become soft, gentle, quiet and relaxed. Follow the breathing in the belly for several breath cycles.

Continue breathing slow and soft and smooth, but shift the attention to the heart center. With each breath imagine breathing love, joy or compassion into the heart.

Use a memory of a time you have felt a strong positive emotion as a tool to help you feel deeply and strongly. You might also imagine breathing in a healing color into the heart: white, gold or violet.

Place a very slight grin on the face and smile down to the heart. Notice any sensations in the heart or chest area. Can you feel the heart expanding and opening?

Create a clear image of a friend, family member or romantic partner in your mind. Imagine sending the love and compassion you have generated toward them. You may wish to hold the hands up in front of the body, palms facing out to enhance the feeling of sending energy.

Find the words to express what you wish for that individual

> "May you be healthy and happy"
> "May you be safe and protected"
> "May you find peace"

As much as possible, experience the feelings associated with these wishes. Allow them to fill your entire being.

Continue choosing subjects for your open heart practice until the end of the meditation.

You may also want to send specific wishes, feelings or intentions to all beings, specific regions of the world that are in conflict or handling a natural disaster, the planet Earth, or to the 4 directions.

Note: Many forms of Open Heart meditation incorporate the practice of sending positive feelings and intentions to the self. Sometimes this is done at the beginning and/or end of the meditation or it may be the entire focus of the practice. While this can be a very powerful practice, it is also sometimes difficult for someone in the midst of a depressive episode.

OPEN HEART MEDITATIONS AND FRONTAL LOBE ASYMMETRY

Brain imaging research consistently demonstrates that Open Heart practices engage regions of the brain involved in sustained attention and emotional processing (Hoffmann, et al., 2011). While a comprehensive exploration of all the brain regions involved in an Open Heart practice is beyond the scope of this chapter, it is important to note that the left prefrontal cortex of the brain is consistently among them (other brain regions commonly involved are discussed in the box labeled, "Open Heart Meditation and the Brain: The Research").

OPEN HEART MEDITATION AND THE BRAIN:
THE RESEARCH

- Lutz and colleagues (2008) demonstrated that Lovingkindness-Compassion meditations consistently activate specific brain regions known to be involved in the perception of another's emotional state. Two areas in particular, the right anterior insula and the ACC have been found to be related to empathy for others suffering and are activated in both novice and experienced meditators when they are engaged in a compassion meditation.

- Tarrant et al., (2015) found that experienced meditators listening to a guided Twin Hearts Meditation showed significant increases in gamma activity in the right insula, anterior cingulate cortex (ACC) and left medial frontal gyrus. Novice meditators showed inconsistent patterns of activation in these areas. In addition, experienced meditators from this tradition were found to have higher self-reported happiness and lower levels of anxiety than the novice group.

- Other research has shown that both experienced and empathic pain activate the ACC and insula, supporting the notion that they are important in subjective feeling states (Craig, 2009; Singer et al., 2004).

- It has been noted by Craig (2009) that most studies examining activation patterns of the anterior insula, also observe activation of the ACC. Joint activation of the ACC and Insula supports the idea that these two areas largely serve as complementary regions that work together with few exceptions.

Engstrom (2010) presented data on a Tibetan Buddhist with many years of compassion meditation practice. During meditation, fMRI imaging revealed activation of several brain regions involved in sustained attention and empathy. However, the strongest findings were related to activation of the left prefrontal cortex. In a study comparing eight long-term meditators with eight novice meditators, there were common activation patterns found in the adepts when engaged in an Open Heart form of meditation. Among the findings, expert meditators showed large increases in gamma brainwave activity during the meditation in several areas of the brain including the *left prefrontal cortex*. Interestingly, the monks with the most experience showed the strongest patterns while the novice meditators showed only very minor increases in gamma power (Lutz et al., 2004).

BRAIN REGIONS INVOLVED IN **OPEN HEART MEDITATIONS**

Anterior Cingulate Gyrus (or Anterior Cingulate Cortex)

This region of the brain serves as a connection between the higher brain centers of the cortex and the lower brain centers of the limbic system. As such it is very important in coordinating elements of thinking and feeling. The ACC is involved in many tasks, one of which is the ability to sustain attention.

Insula

The insulae are believed to be involved in cognitive-emotional processes such as empathy and self-aware emotional feelings. This is supported by functional imaging results showing that the structure and function of the right frontal insula are correlated with the ability to feel one's own heartbeat, the experience of basic emotions including anger, fear, disgust, happiness and sadness as well as the ability to empathize with the pain of others (Phan, 2002).

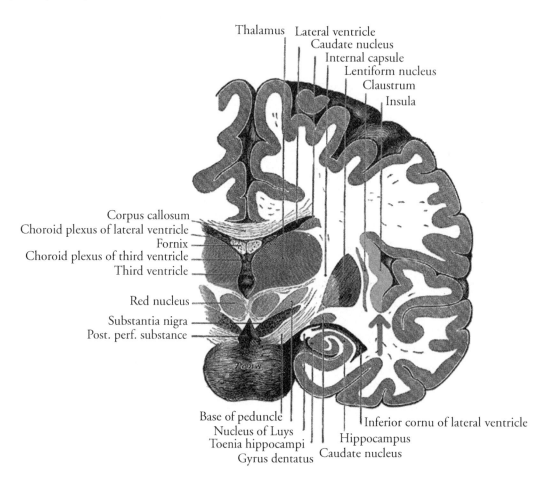

Taken together, these studies provide compelling evidence that Open Heart practices can have an important impact on psychological and emotional symptoms AND these improvements may be more significant with increased practice. Based on everything we know about brain plasticity, this makes perfect sense; the more you exercise certain structures and functions of the brain, the stronger they become.

While these findings lend support to the idea that Open Heart practices can be used to shift the brain into a more positive, optimistic pattern there are additional factors to consider.

When a 15-minute Open Heart meditation was compared to a 15-minute Focus meditation, the results were not exactly what we might expect. The subjects in this study had a history of depression and no significant meditation practice. The researchers measured frontal alpha asymmetry before and after the meditations to determine the impact on brain activation patterns (Barnhofer, et al., 2010).

Interestingly, the results found that the two different forms of meditation were equally successful at activation patterns toward the left. On the surface this would seem to be a very positive finding-everybody benefits, regardless of meditation type. However, upon closer examination, it was discovered that subjects with higher levels of negative rumination, or brooding, were less successful at using the Open Heart meditation, but were more successful at the Focus practice. Those with lower levels of brooding had the reverse pattern (Barnhofer, et al., 2010).

These results suggest that people who are depressed (brooding) simply may not be able to generate the feeling states necessary for an Open Heart meditation. It is "too far" away from their current state. In some ways, this is like telling someone that is clinically depressed to try feeling better. If you are unable to shift into a positive emotional state, experiencing feelings of appreciation, gratitude or love, it makes sense that practices emphasizing this will not be particularly helpful. In fact, it is possible that they could actually increase feelings of depression by highlighting the thing you are unable to achieve or feel, which brings up an important point about this form of meditation. For Open Heart practices to be effective, you have to feel the feelings. It is not enough to simply think positive thoughts or repeat specific phrases of lovingkindness. Those are helpful tools and strategies, but you will not get the same benefit from this practice if you cannot generate the required feeling states.

This still does not explain why this same group of subjects, scoring high in brooding and potentially still depressed, show a positive shift in brain functioning when engaged in a simple Focus form of meditation. Rather than shifting toward a positive feeling state, perhaps focusing on something neutral (like the breath) has the effect of shifting attention away from negative thoughts or feelings. Rather than moving toward the positive, you are moving away from the negative. Doesn't it make sense that shifting away from negative thoughts, and ruminations would also lead to a favorable shift in brain activation?

OPEN HEART
EEG NEUROMEDITATION

Based on the available research and our understanding of the brain circuitry involved, we can utilize neurofeedback in conjunction with these forms of meditation to help the subject find and maintain the desired state of consciousness.

Open Heart forms of meditation appear to involve activation of the anterior insula and ACC as well as left prefrontal regions. In addition, deactivation of the right parietal region may also play a significant role. This provides a range of options to include in an Open Heart neuromeditation practice and may depend on the precise form the meditation takes.

After completing an 18-minute Open Heart meditation with a protocol rewarding gamma at ACC and gamma at right Insula, an experienced meditator who lived in a Buddhist monastery for 8 years, made the following comments:

> "...During the first session (1st 9-minute run), I found the feedback tones quite distracting to the meditative concentration I was trying to achieve. Because of this, I had to put a considerable amount of effort into keeping my concentration on the content of my meditation. Over the course of the session, this became easier to do, and my state of concentration gradually required less effort. At a certain point, I was aware that the tones were relatively constant, and this corresponded to my own feeling at having achieved a degree of meditative stability. At this point, the feedback tones became more supportive to my meditation practice, as I could tell that when a discrete thought or external stimuli caught my attention and distracted me, one of the tones would cut out. This provided effective feedback that my attention had veered, and gave me impetus to put some effort into letting go of the distraction, or consciously bringing it into my meditation.
>
> During the second session (2nd 9-minute run), I could tell that I was beginning with more meditative stability than I had started with in the first one. And the feedback tones seemed to confirm that. During the session, I could once again tell when my attention would become too preoccupied with something, like when someone started talking on the phone in the other room. The feedback tones also indicated this, and once again I had to put some effort into negotiating that phenomena within the meditation, and I found myself using the feedback tones, in part, to do this. Also, when sirens of an ambulance sounded from the street below, my compassion meditation expanded as I found myself incorporating people suffering in this way as subjects of the meditation."

ACC and Insula Gamma during an open heart neuromeditation

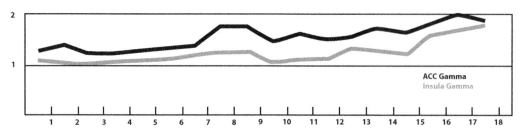

Research examining the relationship between attention and unwanted thoughts sheds some light on this process and provides some direction for us as we consider who might be best served by different forms of meditative practice.

A study published in *Consciousness and Cognition* reported that mind wandering and intrusion of unwanted thoughts were significantly positively correlated with each other (Ju & Lien, 2016). This means that when your mind wanders, your attention is likely to be diverted toward things you don't necessarily want or need to be thinking about. In this particular study, they found that training students to focus on their breathing-learning to shift attention away from mind wandering/intrusive thoughts was an effective strategy in reducing intrusive thoughts. They also found that focusing on the breath was more effective than focusing on specific images at reducing unwanted thoughts and mind wandering. The implications of this research are that focusing attention on the breath might be a particularly useful strategy for those who suffer from depression, anxiety and obsessive-compulsive disorder, since those conditions can erode a person's capacity for mental control.

EXERCISE — **BROODING** SCALE

Instructions: People think and do many different things when they feel depressed. Please read each of the following items and indicate whether you almost never, sometimes, often, or almost always think or do each one when you feel down, sad, or depressed. Please indicate what you generally do, not what you think you should do.

1= Almost Never   2= Sometimes   3= Often   4= Almost Always

1. _____ Think "What am I doing to deserve this?"

2. _____ Think "Why do I always react this way?"

3. _____ Think about a recent situation, wishing it had gone better

4. _____ Think "Why do I have problems other people don't have?"

5. _____ Think "Why can't I handle things better?"

6. _____ Think "Why do I have problems other people don't have?"

7. _____ Think "Why can't I handle things better?"

The Brooding Scale is a subscale of the 71-item Response Styles Questionnaire (RSQ; Nolen-Hoeksema et al., 1993).

EXERCISE — **FOCUS MEDITATION FOR DEPRESSION**

Based on what we know, if someone is in the midst of a depression and perhaps engaged in ruminative, brooding thought patterns, an Open Heart meditation may not be the best initial approach. It may be better to have them engage in a meditation that shifts their attention away from the ruminations. Because Ju & Lien's study (2016) seemed to indicate that focusing on the breath was better than focusing on some other mental image, this may be the preferred strategy. Refer to chapter 2 for specific breath focused meditation instructions. Here are some variations that may be particularly beneficial if using this form of meditation with someone dealing with depression. These strategies are often very helpful in beginning to shift the heart into a more open state and they do not require that the person experience feelings of love, compassion or gratitude.

1. **Heart Focus:** While focusing on the breath, imagine breathing healing energy into and out of the heart center. This does not need to be focused on the area of the physical heart, but rather the center of the chest.

   a. Place a very slight grin on the face and imagine smiling down to the heart

   b. Imagine a healing light in the heart that grows with each inhalation. Colors such as white, gold and purple may be ideal. This light may also be in the form of a flame.

2. **Three-fold Flame:** While focusing on the heart (physical heart), imagine that there is a three-limbed flame in the heart, like a fleur de lis. For each inhale, focus on tracing one branch of the flame from the root to the tip, as if the breath were filling and activating that branch of the flame. Begin with the branch toward your left arm. On the exhale, mentally trace back from the tip to the root. On the next breath, shift attention to the center branch and then for the third breath, mentally trace the branch toward your right arm.

   a. Use physical movements to facilitate focus

      i. Place the thumb, index and middle fingertips together

      ii. Using the grouped fingertips, trace in front of the heart area with each breath

   b. Imagine that each branch has a specific color:

      i. Left branch: blue

      ii. Center branch: gold

      iii. Right branch: pink

   c. With each breath, breathe an intention-as aspect of heart power into each branch:

      i. Left branch: Power or Strength

      ii. Center branch: Wisdom

      iii. Right branch: Beauty of Love

Note: The three-fold flame meditation was originally a part of the Masonic and Rosicrucian traditions. It has more recently been used, in slightly modified form, by the Ascended Master Teachings. Thanks to Tom Williams for his instruction and education in these matters.

STRATEGIC USE OF
DISTRACTIONS

Focusing on the breath is not the only way to suppress unwanted thoughts. Other studies suggest distracting activities can produce positive results. Some clients find that postponing the unwanted thought—allocating 30 minutes to mentally dealing with it later that day or week—can help.

If you or a client are working to manage brooding or a tendency to focus on the negative, it is a good idea to explore a variety of activities to use as tools to shift the mind away from the negative ruminations. Here are some suggestions:

- Exercise
- Gardening
- Arts or Crafts
- Cooking
- Home Improvement Projects
- Take a Class/Learn Something New

You will notice that these suggestions do not include watching television or using drugs/alcohol. While these are probably the most common ways people use distraction, they tend to increase the problem. Choose a distraction that results in some kind of concrete outcome. You are likely to get additional benefit if it involves movement/exercise and if it is outdoors.

Other research examining the impact of Focus meditations on depression and brain activation patterns has found that even a relatively short term practice alters frontal alpha asymmetry in a direction associated with more positive emotion (Moyer, et al, 2011). Thus, to optimize success, the type of meditation utilized may depend on symptom expression and personality characteristics (Bernhardt & Singer, 2012; Stinson & Arthur, 2013).

If a client is in the midst of a significant depression, beginning their meditation training with an Open Heart practice may not be the best fit. In fact, it might even increase their level of discouragement. For someone currently battling a depressive episode, it might make more sense to teach them strategies to shift the mind away from the negative thoughts (Focus practices) along with supplemental strategies for beginning to increase the brain's capacity to experience positive emotional states. As the person recovers from the depression, that might be a better time to introduce Open Heart meditations.

OPEN HEART MEDITATION TIP #1:
CREATE AN ENVIRONMENT

It is important to consider the role of the environment in your practice. What elements of your practice space could facilitate entering an open, loving, generous state of consciousness?

- **Cleanliness:** In general, people tend to feel more relaxed in a tidy space. Remove clutter and keep your practice area neat and organized.

- **Beauty:** Find pictures, art, figurines or other decorations that represent beauty to you and keep these in your area. You could also keep fresh flowers in the space.

- **Music:** Play soft background music during your meditative practice that will facilitate this state. Perhaps it is associated with a religious/spiritual tradition or kirtan chanting or Native American flute music.

- **Altar:** Create an altar for your space. This does not have to be religious or spiritual, but serves as a center point for your practice. You may use this as a way to simply display beauty with candles and flowers. You might also place pictures of loved ones, spiritual figures or other meaningful objects. Make this your own. Don't worry about what you think an altar is "supposed" to look like. Does it represent you and your practice?

OPEN HEART MEDITATION TIP #2:
UNPLUG TO REDUCE NEGATIVITY

Most television programs (including the news) are written to stir powerful uncomfortable feelings. This is a tactic to keep your attention and it works! Unfortunately, the brain responds to these images and messages by initiating a stress response. Even if the images and stories are clearly false, the brain often responds as if it were true.

As discussed earlier in this chapter, sometimes moving away from negative stimuli is just as important as moving toward positive stimuli. Answer these questions and challenge yourself to reduce the negative influences in your life.

1. Think about the information you receive throughout the day in the form of television, news, video gaming, the Internet and social media.

2. How much of this information is negative or causes you to feel upset, distressed, frightened or angry?

3. The next time you turn on the news or log in to Facebook, become mindful of the impact of the messages you see, read and hear. How do they affect your thoughts, feelings and body?

4. Ask yourself if the information you are ingesting is helpful. Does it help you to become a better person?

5. Make a conscious decision to limit, minimize or eliminate the sources of information that are not beneficial.

6. Be specific. What limits will you set?

For example:
    a. "I will only check Facebook for 10 minutes of my lunch hour"
    b. "If I notice myself becoming agitated while watching the news I will turn it off"
    c. "I will not take my phone with me on walks or during meals"

OPEN HEART MEDITATION TIP #3:
USE YOUR WORDS

You will notice in many forms of Open Heart meditation that there are specific phrases used to focus the mind and assist in evoking a specific positive emotional state. Below are two ways you can easily incorporate this into your practice. However, I also encourage you to find the words and language that fits best for you.

1. Metta Phrases:

   a. While focusing your attention on a specific person, region of the country or issue repeat the following phrases while attempting to generate the emotional state that is evoked:

   - May you be safe and free from harm
   - May you be well in body and mind
   - May you be happy and filled with peace

2. Modified Prayer of St. Francis of Assisi:

   a. Say the prayer out loud or in your mind. Linger with each line of the prayer, tuning in to that specific feeling state and adding additional lovingkindness wishes for specific people, regions or concerns:

   - Make me an instrument of peace.

   - Where there is hatred, let me sow love;

   - Where there is injury, pardon;

   - Where there is doubt, faith;

   - Where there is despair, hope;

   - Where there is darkness, light;

   - Where there is sadness, joy.

EXERCISE — **DAILY COMPASSION PRACTICES**

In addition to a formal daily meditation practice, exercises that actively engage the feeling states of compassion and lovingkindness throughout the day can be very important. Try these:

1. **Peace be with you and with me:** Throughout the day as you pass by people in your life, think to yourself "peace be with you" or "may you be blessed" or some other similar phrase. Attempt to send feelings of peace and acceptance to everyone you see. Opportunities to practice this are everywhere and can include sitting in the coffee shop, walking through the grocery store, or passing other cars on the highway.

2. **Witnessing the heart of others:** When you encounter others, visualize a strong purple flame in their heart, burning bright. This is a great practice to use when meeting someone for the first time or when addressing a group of individuals. I frequently use this before giving a workshop; visualizing a bright purple flame in each person in the room. This practice is similar to greeting people with the Indian phrase, "Namaste" which roughly translates into "the divine in me recognizes the divine in you."

3. **Remembering the Child:** As you are watching others, noticing any judgments you may have about them, can you recognize that they were once small helpless children. Can you "see" them as a baby in your mind? Can you recognize their sweet quality? Can you see them as a parent might see a child? Can you recognize that this is still part of who they are now?

SUPPLEMENTAL STRATEGIES

Obviously, if someone is depressed or working to manage mood related concerns, it is vital to help them begin to experience more positive and neutral emotional states. While we have already discussed the role that a Focus meditation may play in this process, it is important to consider additional strategies to assist the brain in beginning to spend more time with left frontal activation and less time with right frontal activation.

ENVIRONMENTAL **SUPPORT**

If the goal is to experience more joy, love, gratitude and generosity, it makes sense to involve additional lifestyle changes to support this work. Here are a few suggestions:

1. **Move Your Body:** Exercise that is aerobic (running) and/or involves complex movements (Taiji Chuan, dancing) have been linked to significant improvements in the treatment of anxiety, depression and other mood disorders. In addition, exercise and meditation both facilitate the growth of neurons in the hippocampus.

2. **Spend Time in Nature:** Research has clearly shown that people who spend time outside in sunny, green and natural spaces tend to be happier and healthier than those that do not (Bratman et al., 2015).

3. **Sleep:** There are over 200 studies showing a clear relationship between sleep problems and depression. While sleep problems may be the result of depression, behavioral treatments that regulate the sleep rhythm have a proven effectiveness when managing mood disorders (Berk, 2009).

ACCESSING "POSITIVE" OR PLEASANT EMOTIONS

For persons dealing with mood concerns, accessing positive emotions may be an important, but challenging part of their recovery. As research with depressed people has shown, someone in the midst of a depressive episode is likely to have difficulty tapping in to feelings such as "lovingkindness." In fact, feelings like "love," "compassion," and "joy" may feel too big and too far away for them to access. Because of this, it is often a good idea to help people tune into positive emotional states that have less intrinsic intensity, such as appreciation.

Appreciation is often a good entry point for people attempting to access a positive emotional state. It can be described as a blend of thankfulness, admiration, approval and gratitude. When pressed, most everyone can find something to be appreciative for, even if it is as simple as the weather outside or the end of a work day. The important thing with this work is to activate and experience the emotion. Thinking the thought, "I appreciate the Spring weather" is great, but is nowhere near as powerful as actually experiencing the feeling of appreciation in the heart. This same issue is true when dealing with gratitude or any other positive emotional state.

OPENING **THE HEART**

For people that have difficulty experiencing positive feelings, this work can be very uncomfortable. When a basic practice like working with appreciation proves to be challenging, ask them to try some of these practices instead:

- Breathing in and out of the heart center
- Using imagery (gold light)
- Smiling down to the heart
- Imagine being surrounded by loved ones/spiritual being(s)
- "Safe/Secure place" imagery

Remember, at this point, you are simply attempting to help them experience a more positive emotional state which can be challenging for many people. These introductory practices can have powerful effects on gently opening the heart to allow for the experience of larger, more powerful feeling states. As someone begins this work, it is possible that they may experience some "side effects" including emotionality, crying, being easily "touched" by emotion in others or the sensation of an aching heart. These are all normal experiences that accompany the letting down of defenses.

USE A **MEMORY**

When working with someone that has difficulty finding something to be appreciative or grateful for, it can be very useful to help them find a memory they can use as a positive emotional anchor.

The memory can be of anything that evokes a strong positive emotion. For example, my "go to" memory is being present when my son was born. Even though it was many years ago, the intensity of the emotion from that time can still be felt.

Most people have at least one strong positive memory they can tap in to when they need help shifting into a more positive place.

Importantly, it does not matter that the event is not current. Like the stress response, the brain does not necessarily distinguish between past, present and future. If you see the image in your mind, the brain will respond as if it is real.

APPRECIATION **BREAKS**

1. Set an alarm to "go off" at a specified time during the day or several times throughout the day.

   a. Or, download and use the mindfulness bell app for your phone.

2. When the alarm goes off, take a break from what you are doing.

3. Take a few slow, deep breaths.

4. See what you can appreciate RIGHT NOW in this moment.

5. Enhance this feeling by mentally explaining to yourself why you are appreciative.

6. Put a grin on your face.

7. Experience the feeling in the heart and allow it to expand.

This entire practice can be done in 30 seconds. It is a great strategy to bring these practices into our daily lives and disrupt the hurried, negative, rat race mentality we often find ourselves in.

Just imagine what it would be like if we all did this 3 times each day.

AN ATTITUDE OF GRATITUDE

Gratitude can generally be defined as being thankful and full of appreciation. It has been studied extensively for its ability to help people shift into a more positive emotional state and is often a primary component of prayer. In her book *Bouncing Back*, Linda Graham reports that people who have a daily gratitude practice are more likely to experience a whole list of benefits including: more positive emotions, higher likelihood of achieving goals, better sleep, lower blood pressure, longer lives and feeling more alert, energetic, enthused, alive (2013). Not a bad list! But what does it mean to "practice gratitude?" How can we intentionally engage this attitude?

EXERCISE — GRATITUDE **JOURNAL**

1. Find a place to be quiet and alone for 5 minutes

2. Write down 3 things that you truly feel grateful for in your life

3. For each item, explain WHY you feel grateful

4. As you engage in the exercise attempt to tune in to the feelings of gratitude

   a. Where in your body do you experience it?

   b. How would you describe the feeling?

   c. Does the feeling have a color or texture?

5. Repeat this exercise every day (or as often as possible)

Step 3 of this exercise is critical. Many versions of this exercise leave this part out which makes it too easy to simply make a list without experiencing the feelings. When you explain why you feel grateful, it forces you to engage in a deeper way with the exercise.

Variation: Write down 3 (or 5) good things that happened to you today (and why they were good)

Bonus: After completing the exercise read each item out loud, with your hand on your heart and a smile on your face.

Double Bonus: Do this before bed each night and notice how it helps you sleep better.

EXERCISE — THANK YOU **LETTER**

1. Take a few minutes to think about someone that has done something you appreciate.

   a. Someone that has had a significant impact on your life

   b. Someone you would like to thank

   c. Someone you appreciate having in your life

   d. Someone that has done something kind or generous for you

2. Write a letter with specific details about what it is you appreciate.

3. Intentionally connect with the feelings of gratitude and appreciation while writing the letter.

Bonus: Send the letter to the person.
Double-Bonus: Read the letter out loud to the person!

EXERCISE — PRAYER AS
GRATITUDE

Many people think of prayer as asking God for something they want or need-either for themselves or someone they love. However, prayer can simply be an opportunity to give thanks for what you already have and does not necessarily have to be a religious or spiritual practice.

1. **Meal-time:** Take a moment before eating your meal and simply recognize the amount of energy and work that it took to make this food available for you. Can you be grateful for that energy and work? You might use a statement such as this: "I am grateful for all the energy it took to make this food available for me. Thank you to the sun, the Earth, the rain. Thank you to the farmers that planted, cultivated and harvested this food. Thank you to the various workers that transported the food and made it available for me. Thank you for all that energy; may it be fully absorbed into my body to nurture me, allowing me to help others."

2. **Beginning of the Day:** Take a moment soon after waking in the morning-maybe even while still in bed-to feel gratitude for having another day. You might use a statement such as this: "I am grateful for another day on this Earth. For another day to enjoy this body. I am grateful for the opportunity to bring light and joy to others."

3. **End of the Day:** Take a moment just before bed-maybe even while in bed-to feel gratitude for the day you just experienced. You might use a statement such as this: "I am grateful for this day. I am grateful for the joys and the challenges. I appreciate what I have learned and I trust that this day will make me a better person tomorrow." You might also reflect on specific events from the day that you appreciate or were grateful for.

DEEPENING THE POSITIVE

It is an interesting and unfortunate fact that humans seem to be wired for negativity. Think about it. Notice how much time and energy you are willing to put on even slightly negative events that happen during the day, but how little attention you place on positive events. As an example of this process try this thought experiment:

> *"Imagine you are walking down the hall at work and are passing by a co-worker who is walking the other direction. This is someone you know, but are not really friends with-a work acquaintance. Let's imagine that, as you pass by you look up and smile at them. Imagine that they look up and frown at you."*

In this imaginary scenario, it is very likely that you will immediately begin scanning for things you might have said or done in the recent future that could have caused this person to be upset with you. Did you step on their toes in some way? Did you interfere with a project they were working on? Did you say or do something that could have been offensive? You might start worrying about future meetings you have with this person. You might contemplate going to talk to them to see if you can mend the situation. In fact, you might still be thinking about this situation while lying in bed that night."

OK. Now imagine this scenario:

> *"Imagine you are walking down the hall at work and are passing by a co-worker who is walking the other direction. This is someone you know, but are not really friends with—a work acquaintance. Let's imagine that, as you pass by you look up and smile at them. Imagine that they look up and smile at you."*

How long do you think about this interaction? Does it even register? Probably not. This seems to be the way we are as humans. As Rick Hanson says in his book, *Buddha's Brain*, we are Teflon for positive experiences and Velcro for negative experiences (2009). In fact, he sites numerous research studies that quite clearly show that we are physiologically wired for negativity. From an evolutionary perspective, this makes a great deal of sense. If you want to survive as a species, doesn't it make sense that you would focus more on the potential dangers in your environment, rather than the things that might make you feel good? This is precisely what the amygdala is doing a good deal of the time-scanning the environment for negative stimuli. It is a threat analysis machine. While this is a wonderful adaptive mechanism, it often leaves us focused on the things that could go wrong or might be a threat. If we want to experience a more positive outlook, we need to retrain these tendencies. You need to engage the positive experiences in our lives and actively experience them to shift our default negativity focus.

TAKING IN **THE GOOD**

1. Look for or simply notice positive events in your life. These may be internal or external events and can include:

   a. Someone doing something kind or generous

   b. Feeling good

      i. Brain working properly

      ii. Body feeling strong

      iii.Emotionally feeling content or confident

   c. Create your own positive event by doing something kind or generous for someone else.

2. Savor the positive event.

   a. Feel into the event, allowing it to become an emotional experience

   b. Notice sensations in the body

   c. See if you can intensify the feeling

3. Sense and intend that the positive experience is soaking into every cell of your body.

Sometimes we forget to take the time to engage in these practices as they happen during the day. Take a few moments at night-before bed to recall the moments of the day that you were unable to savor and savor them now.

Adapted from *Buddha's Brain* by Rick Hanson (2009)

GETTING THE BODY INVOLVED

Because we are interested in finding complementary interventions to help shift the brain into a more receptive or positive state, it seems important to consider the potential role that the body may play in this process.

POSTURE MATTERS

Researchers exploring the relationship between mood and the body have found that walking in a slouched posture may decrease subjective feelings of energy and increase negative emotions. In fact, subjects walking with a slouched posture reported feelings of "wanting to just sit down," "low energy" and "depressive feelings." Walking in an erect posture and skipping tended to increase subjective feelings of energy and positive emotional states (Peper & Lin, 2012). Similarly, Nair and colleagues found that a slumped posture increased the experience of negative emotional states while an upright posture helped people maintain positive emotional states (Nair et. al, 2015). Other research has demonstrated that it is easier for subjects to access negative thoughts and memories in a slumped position while it is easier to access positive thoughts and memories in an upright position (Tsai, et al., 2016; Wilson & Peper, 2004). Based on this research, the saying, "fake it till you make it" makes a lot of sense. Even though you may be feeling down, shift the body to help the brain shift. What a simple and powerful intervention. Tell your mood what to do!

EXERCISE — **BODY-EMOTION**
MINDFULNESS

The next time you catch yourself feeling sad, depressed, down or fatigued try this:

1. Notice your body: what is your posture? How about your facial expression: How is your body reflecting your current emotional/psychological state?

2. Think of the emotional/psychological state you would rather experience in this moment. Maybe it is courage, confidence, contentment, or gratitude.

3. How would your body be different if you were experiencing that emotional/ psychological state?

4. Change your body posture and facial expression to match the desired state

5. Recall a time that you have experienced the desired feeling/psychological state

6. Attempt to feel and embody that desired state right now.

EXERCISE — OPENING THE HEART:
RESTORATIVE YOGA

One of the physical manifestations of depression is a caved chest. This appears to be a way that the mind/body naturally attempts to protect the heart. Unfortunately, this pattern can often become habitual, leading to defensiveness and an inability to feel positive feelings. Use the following exercise to open the heart area.

Props are helpful. Before you begin you will want to gather a yoga mat (or blanket, camp pad, etc.), a pillow and a yoga bolster (or rolled up towel).

- Lie on the yoga mat/blanket

- Place the bolster/rolled towel under your upper back

- Place the pillow under your head

- Allow the arms to be heavy and fall to the side, palms up

- Bend the knees and place the feet on the floor to protect the lower back

- Breath slowly and gently

- Focus on relaxing the muscles of the body

- Place a soft grin on the face

- Hold the posture for 10 or 15 minutes

Bonus #1-Attempt to generate a positive feeling such as appreciation, gratitude, love, or caring.

Bonus #2-As you breathe, imagine breathing in and out of the heart area.

Bonus #3-Smile down at the heart center.

Chapter 5 — DISORDERS OF THE "SELF": Strategies to Quiet the Mind

THE "SELF" AND MENTAL HEALTH

A common characteristic of many mental health difficulties is a distorted sense of self. In essence, the person is not perceiving themselves accurately and this misperception increases the likelihood of certain feelings and behaviors which in turn reinforce the distorted view.

The distorted ways that people refer to themselves—both internally or externally-- include saying things such as "I'm fat," "I'm stupid," "nobody likes me," or "I will always be an addict." These types of statements become definitions of the self; part of the identity.

While everyone experiences distorted thoughts and feelings, when these distortions become exaggerated, rigid and/or inconsistent, they can lead to a range of serious difficulties. This process happens very clearly in conditions like Anorexia Nervosa. In fact, Anorexia is characterized by a distorted body image. Individuals with this diagnosis perceive themselves as weighing more than they actually do. They "see" themselves as fat even though they may be dangerously underweight.

This kind of extreme distortion is also evident when working with the Personality Disorders and Obsessive Compulsive Disorder. A common characteristic of Personality Disorders is an identity disturbance, described as an illogical, incoherent or inconsistent pattern of thoughts and feelings. In fact, particular Personality Disorders such as Borderline Personality Disorder and Narcissistic Personality Disorder are almost entirely defined by a distorted sense of self.

Both eating and personality disorders are known to be among the most difficult mental health conditions to treat (alongside addictions). The primary mental health treatments used for these concerns often involve some form of cognitive-behavioral therapy. At its most basic, cognitive-behavioral therapy (CBT) is based on the understanding that thoughts, feelings and behaviors are all interconnected. Consequently, when you begin to challenge and change inaccurate thinking, problematic behaviors, and distressing emotional responses, you alter the interaction between the three components, which leads to changes in symptoms.

If a rigid and/or inaccurate view of the self is part of the problem, doesn't it make sense that strategies that would shift or quiet this distorted self-view could be important? When we can minimize or temporarily eliminate the repetitive loop of distorted "selfing," this creates an opportunity for something new to happen. It is a chance to break the cycle.

This book, and this chapter in particular, are focused on meditative strategies that may be used either as a primary or adjunctive strategy for treatment. Because we are interested in strategies that will shift the person away from repetitive self-criticism and worry, the strategies that follow will explore styles of meditation that aid in quieting the mind.

COGNITIVE THERAPY
BASICS

Cognitive therapy and related approaches are an excellent complement to several meditation styles including Mindfulness and Quiet Mind. Learning to de-identify with your thoughts is a key component to both.

The diagram below outlines a basic formula for engaging in cognitive therapy techniques. You will see that it requires the person to step back from their thoughts and examine them from a distance. It challenges the reality of the thoughts and provides a frame for re-examining our tendency to attach significance to everything we think.

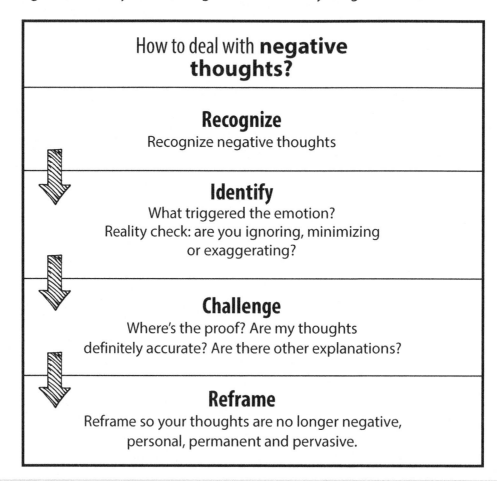

How to deal with negative thoughts?

Recognize
Recognize negative thoughts

Identify
What triggered the emotion?
Reality check: are you ignoring, minimizing or exaggerating?

Challenge
Where's the proof? Are my thoughts definitely accurate? Are there other explanations?

Reframe
Reframe so your thoughts are no longer negative, personal, permanent and pervasive.

QUIET MIND MEDITATIONS

Meditations in the Quiet Mind category involve moving beyond the procedures of the meditation, toward a quiet state of restful awareness. The internal chatter of the conscious mind is minimized and the person in this state often feels a sense of spaciousness and peace. This form of meditation is the stereotype of "meditation." Unlike the other forms of meditation covered in this book, Quiet Mind practices involve learning to let go of mental constructs and drop below the surface of the conscious mind.

TRANSCENDENTAL MEDITATION (TM)

Most research involving the Quiet Mind style of meditation has focused on the practice of Transcendental Meditation (TM; Travis & Shear, 2010). In TM, you begin by engaging the conscious mind in some form of focused attention, such as the use of a mantra. For this reason, TM is sometimes misidentified as a Focus form of meditation. In reality, the focus on a mantra is temporary, and used as a tool to help stabilize the mind. The actual practice of TM reveals that it is a technique for transcending its own procedures; moving from a state of sustained attention to mental silence (Yogi, 1997). As the meditation progresses, the focus shifts and softens so that the mantra becomes part of the background or is dropped altogether in favor of a relaxed spacious awareness.

TM AND BRAINWAVES

TM has been studied extensively and consistently results in increased alpha1 (8-10 hz) power and connectivity (Travis & Shear, 2010). Alpha1 is considered a slow brainwave and is associated with reduced external attention, vigilance and expectancy (Klimesch, et al., 1998; Klimesch, 1999). As we learn to increase alpha1 during a meditative practice, the mind becomes more settled and is less involved in the seeking of stimuli.

While surface brain wave analyses have demonstrated increased alpha1 in a variety of regions including frontal and frontal-parietal connectivity, one study looked deeper into the brain to examine areas where the alpha1 brainwave activity originates.

eLORETA and its associated techniques (sLORETA) use advanced mathematics to calculate the "inverse solution." By using data from surface EEG, this software can extrapolate into deeper brain regions to identify the source of specific brain activity. In this study, 38 subjects were randomly assigned to either learn TM or serve as a control group. At the end of 3 months, all subjects were assessed using a Quantitative EEG. The TM group was evaluated during meditation and the control group was assessed while relaxing with their eyes closed. The results indicated that the TM group showed significant increases in alpha1 activity. This was observed in multiple locations on the surface of the brain and in deeper brain structures associated with the default mode network (DMN; Travis et al., 2010).

QUIET MIND MEDITATION TIP #1:
USE A MANTRA TO STABILIZE THE MIND

A mantra is simply a word or phrase that is repeated as the focus for the meditation. This is a common technique used in Focus practices. It can also be used at the beginning of a Quiet Mind meditation to stabilize the mind. In fact, it is not uncommon to see a variety of meditations begin with focus on the breath or a mantra as a way to help the mind begin to settle before moving on to the "main attraction" of the particular practice.

The mantra used can be any word or phrase that is meaningful to the meditator. It can be something taken from a spiritual/religious tradition, or a specific intention. The mantra can be coordinated with the breath cycle or not. Examples of specific mantras:

- "OM"
- "Om Mane Padme Hum"
- Breathing in "I am safe," breathing out "I am calm"
- "I am, that I am"
- "All is love"
- "I am not the thoughts, I am not the body, I am not the emotions"

QUIET MIND MEDITATION TIP #2:
RELAX THE EYES AND TONGUE

It is a well-known fact that our eyes move when we are "seeing" things in our mind. It is, as if, the eyes are still tracking the visual information even though it is not actually present in the "real" world. The most common example of this occurs during REM (rapid eye movement) sleep where we are dreaming, but also occurs anytime we are visualizing something.

A similar process happens with our tongue when we are thinking in words. When we are "hearing" thoughts in our mind, the tongue makes tiny micro-movements as if it is saying the words.

Most of our thoughts come to us in the form of images and/or words. To help the mind quiet down and reduce internal processing, try relaxing the eyes and tongue during meditation.

1. Maintain a downward gaze
   a. If the eyes are open, keep a soft focus on an area a few feet in front of you on the ground
   b. Do not drop the head; just the eyes. Dropping the head will cause the mind to become sluggish

2. Relax the tongue
   a. Notice tension in the tongue and attempt to let this go
      - The tongue will feel "fat" and float to the back of the mouth

THE **DEFAULT MODE NETWORK** (DMN)

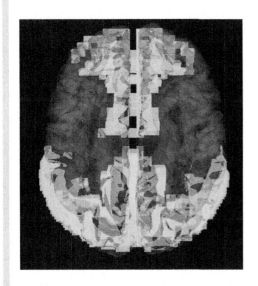

The DMN, as the name implies is a network of brain regions working together to accomplish certain tasks or during specific mental states. When activated, the person is engaged in some level of cognitive processing related to their sense of self. This might be a memory, thinking of others, or simply thinking about his or her self. Depending on the specific type of mental processing, different regions may be more or less engaged than others. Some of the most common areas engaged in the DMN include the following:

Posterior Cingulate Cortex (PCC): The lower part of the PCC actives in all tasks related to the self, related to others, remembering the past, thinking about the future, and processing concepts plus spatial navigation. The upper part of the PCC involves involuntary awareness and arousal.

Medial Prefrontal Cortex (mPFC): This area of the brain becomes active during self-processing such as personal information, autobiographical memories, future goals and events, and decision making regarding those personally very close such as family.

Angular Gyrus: Connects perception, attention, spatial cognition, and action and helps with parts of recall of episodic memories

Image of default mode network using sLORETA analyses in BrainAvatar software, BrainMaster Technologies, Inc.

The fact that the DMN shuts down (increased alpha1) in this type of meditation is central to its impact because the DMN is very much involved in the creation and repetition of stories about the self. Here's how it works: When a person is externally focused on some type of goal directed behavior, like writing a paper or balancing the checkbook, the default mode network is quiet. During these times, a different brain network is often engaged, called the salience network. However, as soon as the person is done with their task, the mind shifts to its default state. This is where it goes when it is not doing something else. Interestingly, our default state is to think about ourselves or something in relation to ourselves. Consider the reality of this for a moment; when you take a break from work or are engaged in some "mindless" activity what are you thinking about? You might be thinking about your next meal, or the fact that your back hurts, or your grocery list, or your parents. Whatever you are thinking about is about you and your sense of self. At its most basic level, when you are not doing something else, you are thinking about yourself or something in reference to yourself. During these times, your default mode network is activated.

OK, so humans are self-centered. This is probably not news to anyone. But what if your sense of self is distorted or rigid or inconsistent? What if your sense of self creates serious difficulties and distress for you on an almost continual basis? What if you are suffering from OCD or an eating disorder or a Personality Disorder? In these cases, it might be very useful to quiet down that constant self-referencing. It might be a very powerful experience to let go of the distorted "selfing." This appears to be what is happening in Quiet Mind practices such as TM.

Based on this understanding, Quiet Mind forms of meditation may be best for psychological disorders involving disruptions in a sense of self. Interestingly, some neurofeedback practitioners have already begun using a form of this training when working with challenging mental health conditions. Mark Smith, an international neurofeedback instructor, reported that he has had tremendous success treating addictions and Personality Disorders by using a neurofeedback protocol that involves rewarding alpha activity in the Precuneus. Because the Precuneus is the hub of the Default Mode Network, increased alpha in this region is associated with a quieting of the DMN. Smith reported that this form of neurofeedback produces a "calm sense of integrity" in his clients with Personality Disorder diagnoses (personal communication, January 14, 2013).

Whether you are quieting the mind and the DMN through meditation or neurofeedback, this process can be very powerful for individuals with a poor sense of self. Quieting the illogical or distorted perceptions of self allows for a broader perspective, which is beneficial in the development of a healthy ego. There is additional evidence for this idea in a study which found that higher levels of thought-action fusion were positively correlated to activation of the Precuneus (Jones & Bhattacharya, 2014).

Thought-action fusion is very common in OCD, but is also present in other mental health concerns such as anxiety and depression. It is the belief that thinking a particular thought increases the likelihood that the thought will actually happen. A common example of thought-action fusion relates to beliefs around worrying. It is common for people with some level of anxiety to believe that worrying (thought) will prevent something bad from happening (action). Because this type of thinking is always referenced to the person having the thought, it always involves the DMN. So, imagine the impact of shutting down the DMN. You can't have these types of thoughts without the DMN so, naturally, if you quiet the DMN it eliminates the possibility of thinking in this manner.

SCRIPT — **BASIC TRANSCENDENTAL MEDITATION** (TM)

Before beginning, make sure you have taken some time to prepare the environment. The state you are seeking is a very quiet, open, spacious place. What environmental triggers can help you shift into this type of consciousness (see box titled, "Choose Your Surroundings").

Choose a mantra to use during your practice. Select this in advance so you can avoid shifting into a left brained decision making process when the meditation begins. Choose something simple, but meaningful to you.

Become physically comfortable. While it is generally not ideal to lie down when meditating, if you have a busy brain and are not at risk of falling asleep, this may be appropriate. If, on the other hand, you tend to doze off as soon as you begin to relax, you will want to choose a posture that allows you to be relaxed but still conscious.

Spend a few moments connecting with the entirety of the body. Can you feel the solidity of your being right now? Hold this awareness for a moment while you take several slow, long, easy, relaxed breaths.

Focus on the breathing in the belly. Allow it be soft, gentle and natural. Just easy slow breaths as the body and mind begin to settle, begin chanting your mantra. Say it out loud in a conversational volume. Listen to your words. Find your rhythm. It can be helpful to create a sing-song rhythm to your mantra. Allow the speaking and the sound of your voice become your focus.

After several minutes, gently begin to quiet the voice.

After several additional minutes, allow the volume to be reduced to a whisper, barely audible to yourself. Anyone else in the room would not even know you were speaking.

Now, allow the chanting to become internal. There is no outward expression. No speech, simply hearing the repetition of the mantra in your mind.

Allow this internal repetition to become quieter, more gentle.

Until. . .

There is silence. . .

Rest in the silence. If the mind begins to stir, see if you can gently shift your mind back to the silence. Become familiar with this space and allow it.

If the mind becomes busy again, return to repeating the mantra aloud and follow the same process, allowing the timing to direct itself.

ZEN

As a quieting of internal mentation is a goal of Quiet Mind meditation practices, it is logical to assume that involving more of the DMN would help to enhance this state. So far we have only discussed the Precuneus as the hub of the DMN. Another primary component of the DMN is the Medial Prefrontal Cortex (MFC) which is involved in processing certain forms of personal information like autobiographical memories and future goals and events. Damage to this portion of the network has been shown to produce an absence of spontaneous thought and a sensation of "mental emptiness" (Damasio & Van Hoesen, 1983), precisely the state we are looking for.

Consistent with this concept of a quiet mind and "internal emptiness," Zen meditators often practice meditative states called "no mind." From a spiritual perspective, the idea is to quiet the voice of the personality-the small mind, so that you can hear the subtle voice of a higher mind-big mind. This type of practice can be thought of as learning to move beyond the personality. Again, this could be particularly helpful if the personality is disturbed in some way.

Research examining brainwave patterns during Zen meditation has consistently shown that the Zen brain is characterized by increases in alpha power, a slowing of the alpha frequency and alpha activity spreading frontally (Kasamatsu & Hirai, 1966; Murata et al., 2004; Takahashi et al., 2005). All of these Zen brainwave patterns are consistent with a mind that is relaxed, alert and quiet.

The description of both the meditative state and the brain wave processes involved in Zen practices appear to have much in common with TM as well as a more modern approach to Quiet Mind meditations.

QUIET MIND **CONTRAINDICATIONS**

While it makes sense that this style of meditation could be helpful for nearly any type of mental health concern, there are a few instances, in which it may be contraindicated.

Dissociation: With clients that already have a tendency to dissociate, this form of practice is inappropriate. For these clients, it may be better to begin with a Focus or Mindfulness meditation.

Strong Attachment to Self: With clients that have a very strong attachment to their identity, Quiet Mind meditations might be disturbing or alarming. It may feel as if they are "losing themselves." For these clients, it may be better to begin with a Mindfulness meditation.

Depression and/or ADHD: Many individuals with depressive and ADHD symptoms have an excess amount of slow brainwave activity. Because Quiet Mind practices tend to increase slow brainwaves, these practices could aggravate symptoms. For these clients, begin with Focus meditation.

OPEN FOCUS MEDITATION AND ALPHA SYNCHRONY

In the late 1960's, Les Fehmi was studying the role that synchronous brain wave activity may play in perception and the processing of information. Because synchronous activity is most prominent in the alpha band, this became the focus of his research. Fehmi created an EEG monitoring system and began experimenting with ways to encourage the brain toward the production of alpha. After 2 weeks of failed attempts, Fehmi finally gave up. At the point that he stopped trying, when his focus and attention relaxed, this was when his alpha increased and became synchronous (Fehmi & Robbins, 2007).

Fehmi had inadvertently discovered that the best way to produce alpha was to let go of that goal. When we use mental effort to control the mind, in a narrow, focused form of attention, the mind is active and engaged. It wants to solve problems and make decisions. When we let go of control, when we allow the attention to be spacious and easy, the mind relaxes.

Fehmi began using neurofeedback to teach himself and others how to find this state of alpha synchrony. He would measure 5 different brain regions and provide an auditory reward when all 5 showed simultaneous increases in alpha. He observed that after this training, people often experienced feelings of peace, increased presence, heightened senses, an ability to see "the big picture," and enhanced creativity. He began experimenting with different mental tricks designed to help the brain enter this state when he stumbled upon a technique he termed, "objectless imagery." Simply put, when the attention is placed on the absence of something using concepts of space, distance and volume, the mind tends to become quiet. Phrased another way, when you focus on nothing, there is nothing for the mind to focus on!

When describing the practice of Open Focus, Fehmi states, "objectless imagery-the multisensory experience and awareness of space, nothingness, or absence almost always elicits large amplitude and prolonged periods of phase-synchronous alpha activity" (Fehmi & Robbins, 2007, p. 36) which appears to have a significant healing effect for many brains and many conditions.

QUIET MIND MEDITATION TIP #3: **SURRENDER**

It is common for beginning Quiet Mind meditators to feel that they have failed when they are unable to find any internal silence during their practice.

Inevitably, these meditators are attempting to quiet the mind by pushing out any thoughts they may have.

While this may seem like the obvious approach, it never works!

Attempting to force the thoughts away often leads to the thoughts rebounding with more strength.

The only way to move to a place of "no thought" is to sink and surrender; let go.

You may recognize the presence of thoughts, just practice not engaging them.

Allow the mind to relax and drift into deeper states of consciousness.

Don't worry about the thoughts, they will quiet on their own without your imposing your will and effort.

This surrender, this letting go, this is the key to Quiet Mind meditation.

EXPERIENCING **OBJECTLESS IMAGERY**

In his book, The Open Focus Brain (2008), Fehmi provides a variety of guiding questions to help people tune in to the volume and distance within and around the body. He tends to focus on the hands and face. In the examples below, I have expanded Fehmi's focus to include the experience of space itself.

Face
- "Can you imagine the distance between your eyes?"
- "Can you imagine the space within your ears?"
- "Can you imagine the space inside your mouth and cheeks?"

Hands
- "Is it possible for you to imagine the space between your right thumb and right index finger?"
- "Can you imagine the space between all fingers on your right hand at the same time?"
- "Can you imagine the distance between all fingers on both hands at the same time?"

Space
- "Can you visualize yourself floating, weightless in the vastness of space?"
- "Can you sense the distance between your body, floating in space and the next star or planet?"
- "Can you allow yourself to be surrounded by the silence and darkness that space provides?"

IF QUIET MIND IS GOOD FOR SO MANY THINGS, WHY BOTHER WITH THE **OTHER 3 STYLES?**

Good question! Remember, not all brains are built the same and not all brains need the same thing. Two of the styles covered in this book are activating (Focus and Open Heart) and two are quieting (Mindfulness and Quiet Mind). If you already have a tendency toward a quiet mind (traditional ADHD, depression), engaging in Quiet Mind meditations may not be the best practice for you. In fact, it could make someone more depressed or lethargic. This is why it is a good idea to consider your goals before choosing a meditation style!

SUPPLEMENTAL STRATEGIES

Because the practice of Quiet Mind is largely about learning to sink below the level of thought, to experience spaciousness and peace, it is important to practice these skills in as many ways as possible. This is particularly true for those who have a very busy mind, a mind plagued by self-criticism, ruminations or negativity. If Quiet Mind is the practice that someone is working with, consider using some of these additional strategies to supplement any formal practice.

Negative Space

Negative space is the space between objects, parts of an object, or around an object(s). It is a concept often used by visual artists to examine the structure of a painting or drawing. Negative space is often used in a very conscious way in art to convey a particular feeling or to challenge the viewer's perspective. In the book, *Drawing on the Right side of the Brain*, Edwards explains this concept through an iconic image seen in Bugs Bunny cartoons (2012). In those cartoons, Bugs would run through a closed door leaving a bunny-shaped hole. That hole is negative space; it conveys something by absence. The objectless imagery described in the use of Open Focus and alpha synchrony training is largely drawing our attention to the negative space. Practice this perspective shifting through a variety of senses.

EXERCISE — VISUAL NEGATIVE SPACE

Negative space usually refers to the absence of something in the visual field. For example, in the image below, the most obvious image is the tree. However, if you tune in to the negative space-the area around the tree, you will also see two faces pointing toward each other. By shifting perspective in this way, you are literally training your brain to become more flexible-to see other options-to let go of preconceived ideas.

Practice looking at negative space in works of art, in magazine pictures and in nature. Aside from the faces in the trunk of the tree below, you can also simply notice the shape of the white areas in the top of the tree. They do not need to be a recognizable shape or anything with meaning, just practice using the eyes to see what is not there.

EXERCISE — **AUDITORY NEGATIVE SPACE**

- **Nature:** Tune in to the sounds in your environment. Notice what you hear. People's voices? Birds singing? The ticking of a clock? Or maybe cars passing by on the road? Now, listen for the absence of those sounds. Listen for the gaps in the noise. Can you hear the sounds of silence?

- **Chanting:** Find an audio recording of chanting or chant yourself without a recording. It may be preferable to choose a simple chant that is repetitive, such as "Om," or "Hu." If you are using a recording, chant along aloud or in your mind. Between chants focus on the absence of sound, the spaciousness.

- There are many such chants available on YouTube. My personal favorite is a recording by Master Choa Kok Sui titled, "OM: the sound of stillness."
This is available at www.pranichealing.net

SCRIPT — **BREATHING NEGATIVE SPACE**

Take a few moments to find a posture that will allow you to breathe easily and freely. A posture that keeps the mind and body relaxed.

Settle into the body, noticing any areas where you might be holding unneeded tension and inviting those areas to let go. Invite those areas to relax just a little more than they are right now.

Bring your attention to your breath.

Feel the breath moving into and out of the lungs.

Notice the belly expanding with each inhalation and contracting with each exhalation.

As you breathe, can you imagine the empty space within your body? Can you see the volume of your abdomen increasing with each inbreath and shrinking with each outbreath, like a balloon filling and emptying of air?

Now, with each breath notice the action of inhalation. Notice the action of exhalation.

Now, notice the space between the inhalation and exhalation; the pause.

Draw your attention to that pause. You might exaggerate it slightly by allowing the breath to "hold" for a count of 3 seconds between each inhalation and each exhalation.

Breathing in. . .

Pause. . .

Breathing out. . .

Pause. . .

Continue in this way, drawing the attention to the absence of breathing action and noticing the quiet and peacefulness of the space between the breath.

EXERCISE — NEGATIVE SPACE WITH THE BODY:
QUIET MIND STANDING QIGONG

In previous chapters, we have examined ways to use basic Qigong practices to assist in achieving different states of consciousness. While the external practice (what the body is doing) may look like the standing meditation described in Chapter 2, the difference is in the attention and intention of the practice. The script from Chapter 2 is included here with additional instructions (highlighted and italicized) emphasizing the change in focus for this practice.

- Stand with your feet shoulder width apart, toes pointing forward.

- Adjust the weight distribution on your feet so that you are perfectly balanced, not learning forward or back. Not leaning to either side.

- Sink the energy of the body into the feet. The feet become heavy, grounded and rooted. It is as if you are a tree and there are roots extending from your feet deep into the Earth. The upper part of the body is empty and free to flow in the breeze.

- Keep the knees slightly bent.

- Notice the tension in the backs of the legs and allow that to relax as much as possible. Use minimal muscles to hold your body in this position.

- Relax the tailbone, allowing it to point down toward the Earth. It is as if you are just beginning to sit into a chair, keeping the back flat without forcing anything. *Imagine that there is an invisible ball of energy just under the buttocks, gently holding you up and supporting the body in this posture. Can you feel the support? Can you rest the body in this posture without using any extra effort?*

- The spine is straight and long. Staying rooted to the Earth, imagine being gently pulled up from the center of the head, as if you are being stretched from the inside.

- Allow the breathing to be slow, long, relaxed and natural in the belly. *Tune in to the cavity of the abdomen. Feel the expanding and contracting of this space with each inbreath and outbreath.*

- Keep the shoulders dropped. If you are not sure, raise the shoulders up toward the ears and then let them go.

- There is a small gap in the armpits. *Imagine a small ball of energy under each arm, gently supporting the arms in this posture. Feel into this space.*

- There is a slight bend in the elbows, wrist and every joint of every finger. *The fingers are separated as if there was a small ball in between every finger. You can feel the slight pressure needed to hold those balls in place without dropping them. Do not use any extra effort, only what is needed. Sense the space between each finger of both hands.*

- The arms float up in front of the body as if you are hugging a tree. The palms of the hands face the heart, the elbows are down, and the shoulders are dropped. *Imagine that you are holding a ball of energy in the arms. Use the least amount of effort possible to hold the ball. Sense the absence in the arms. Can you feel this space?*

- The tip of the tongue rests gently on the roof of the mouth. *Can you sense the volume of the mouth, the space between the rolled tongue and the back of the throat?*

- Relax all the muscles of the face and head.

- Put a very slight grin on your face. So slight that someone watching you may not even see it.

- Hold this posture for as long as you can without creating unnecessary tension. Continually checking in with the body, breath and mind. Any time you find tension in the body, see if you can release it just a little bit more. Remind the breath to stay slow, long and natural in the belly. Keep the mind focused on the empty spaces-between the fingers, under the armpits, between the arms, under the buttocks, in the abdomen and in the mouth. Is it possible to sense into all of these spaces at the same time?

Instructions adapted from the Yi Quan teachings of Master Gao Han (Ken Cohen)

BRAINWAVE STIMULATION

For many people, engaging in TM or Zen-based meditations is challenging. Beginning meditators in these traditions often complain that they do not know if they are doing it right or feel as if they are failing because the mind is active throughout the meditation and they cannot find the "off" switch.

Some people struggle with this form of meditation because they have difficulty generating significant amounts of alpha brainwave activity; their brains simply do not produce enough. Lack of alpha may be a result of a physical or psychological trauma, a family history of substance abuse, or it may just be the way the brain is wired. If the brain struggles with producing alpha, you can imagine how difficult it might be to engage in a meditation where that is the goal.

In these situations, it is often helpful to provide the brain with additional assistance. The process of coaching or guiding the brain into alpha can be facilitated with a variety of brainwave stimulation technologies. At its most basic, these tools work by exposing the brain to specific frequencies to facilitate the brain's production of that same frequency. In this case, exposing the brain to some form of stimulation in the alpha frequency range (8-12 hz).

Here's how it works: When a brief stimulus is presented to the brain, there is a small response in the EEG due to that stimulation (Ciganek, 1961); this is called an evoked response. If you expose the brain to a series of repetitive, successive stimuli within a certain range, the brain will match this rhythm. So, if we were to flash lights in the eyes 10 times per second, the brain would respond with 10 small responses. Ten cycles per second is the speed of brainwaves within the alpha frequency band. So by flashing lights (or sounds or electromagnetic pulses) 10 times each second, you are encouraging the brain to do the same thing.

This type of technology exists in several forms. The most common stimulation technologies describe themselves as "entraining" the brain. This term may not be entirely accurate, but succeeds in describing the desired goal. The most common entrainment technologies use repetitive audio tones that are masked with classical music or nature sounds. The vast majority of meditation CD's on the market that claim to influence brainwaves are using some version of this technology. Other technologies to stimulate the brain include visual stimulation using repetitive flashing lights and low power pulsed electromagnetic frequencies (Pemf) which stimulates the brain directly through the scalp.

By using these technologies in conjunction with meditation, you are gently nudging the brain toward the desired brainwave frequency while practicing the mental skills involved in that state.

AUDIO VISUAL ENTRAINMENT

Audio Visual Entrainment or AVE, as the name implies, uses both sound and light stimulation to impact brainwave patterns. The specially designed glasses have lights built into the eyeset. The glasses and headphones plug into a small controller box which is used to select the program, intensity of light and volume of audio tones. Once you select a program, the lights begin flashing and the tones sound at the identified frequency.

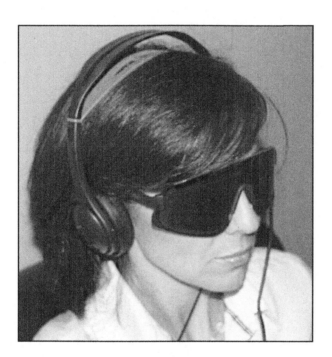

AUDIO VISUAL ENTRAINMENT CASE EXAMPLE:

L., a 36-year-old single mother of two, entered therapy due to extreme emotionality. She reported that she would just start crying for no apparent reason and could not get herself to stop. This began suddenly and without any known environmental trigger. She indicated that she had gone to her physician who did not find anything abnormal in hormone levels.

L's Qeeg showed elevated fast activity in left and right frontal areas.

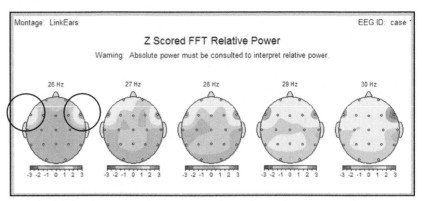

The highlighted areas in these images show elevated activity in frequencies ranging from 26-30hz (beta)

The client was not interested in meditation and did not respond to neurofeedback. We began using alpha brainwave entrainment to help her nervous system relax and become a bit more calm and balanced. The graph below shows her alpha brainwave levels measured toward the back of the head (PZ) for each of 13 sessions.

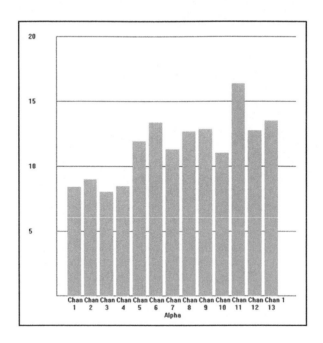

Notice that the alpha levels barely moved during the first 4 sessions. However, at session 5 something interesting happened. The alpha increased significantly and then continued to gradually increase over the remaining sessions. Not surprisingly after around session 7, she reported that her mood had stabilized significantly. She was rarely crying as before. By the end of 13 sessions, she felt that she was "back to normal."

For more information about Brain Wave Stimulation, check out the research, YouTube videos and products at www.MindAlive.com

DOES **BRAIN WAVE ENTRAINMENT (BWE)** REALLY WORK?

Good question! The answer is "yes" and "it depends."

"Yes": The technology behind BWE is sound and has been demonstrated in various formats for many years. Many people will have a tendency to entrain more strongly with one type of stimuli than another. In general, people have a stronger response to visual entrainment than audio entrainment. Of course, using both simultaneously is more powerful than either alone.

"It Depends": While many people respond to BWE in the expected way, others have a different and sometimes opposite response. For example, while many people will show increases in theta brainwaves when stimulating 6-8 hz, others will show a decrease in those frequencies during stimulation. This is because the entrainment from an outside stimuli is creating a response in the brain that is somewhat different than the intrinsic brainwave pattern of the same frequency. Because of this, different brains respond differently. Without using EEG monitoring to see the impact, the best thing to do is try a few devices/frequencies and see how it feels. Does it help you achieve the desired state?

NATURE

Many readers will be familiar with the Safe Place Visualization (on page 135). When you do this exercise, 90-95% of people choose some kind of environment that is nature based; the mountains, ocean or forest. Think about it, where do you go for vacation or to relax on the weekends? Again, if you are like most people you spend time in nature as a way to downshift and feel more grounded.

We are intimately connected to nature and we understand on a very basic level that spending time in nature is important for our health and sense of well-being and science backs this up.

In Japan, there is a practice called Shinrin-Yoku (Forest Bathing) that is sponsored by the government. This practice was designed to encourage the populace to spend time in nature due to the health benefits. Initially, the claims of improved health were based simply on subjective reports. However, since 1990 there have been more than 12 studies conducted to examine the impact of spending time in the Japanese forests. These studies have used both subjective measures as well as objective measure of physiology to confirm what everyone knows intuitively. These researchers have found that time in nature reduces cortisol (stress hormone), lowers blood pressure, increases heart rate variability, reduces psychological stress, depression and hostility, improves sleep and increases feelings of vigor and liveliness.

Other research has demonstrated that simply viewing nature, regardless of the format (plants, poster, slides, video, or virtual reality) has a significant positive impact on the stress response. This reduction in physiological stress has been measured through muscle tension, skin conductance, pulse transit time, cardiac response and hormone levels (Berto, 2014). Based on this data, it should not be surprising that researchers have also found increased alpha brain wave activity when exposed to scenes of nature.

THE BRAIN ON NATURE

Research has shown an increase in alpha brainwaves:

- When viewing slides of natural landscapes versus urban scenes (Ulrich, 1981)
- When viewing plants with flowers versus pots without flowers (Nakamura & Fujii, 1990)
- When watching a green space versus a concrete block fence (Nakamura & Fujii, 1992)

This research and others (see Berto, 2014 for a full review) suggests that spending time in and/or simply viewing nature has a restful and restorative impact on the nervous system. Kaplan explained this through Attention Restoration Theory, arguing that the effortless attention used when we are engrossed in the beauty of nature functions to balance the mental fatigue that occurs from the directed attention that we use throughout our "normal" workday (1995).

Put another way, engaging in a focused, directed type of attention leads to an increase in beta brainwaves (and cognitive overload and stress), while the involuntary, effortless attention we use in nature leads to an increase of alpha brainwaves, allowing the brain to relax and enter a sense of ease and spaciousness.

QUIET MIND AND SPIRITUALITY

If the ego is healthy and mature, this same process of quieting our internal, self-involved stories, may allow us to "let go" and move beyond our sense of self which has become "small" in relation to a broader, more spacious form of consciousness or spirituality. For this reason, Quiet Mind practices may also be a good choice for people seeking connection to something greater than themselves.

EXERCISE — SAFE PLACE
VISUALIZATION

- Take a moment to get comfortable. You may lie down or sit in a comfortable chair.

- Close the eyes and allow the breathing to be full, quiet, soft and relaxed.

- Take a moment to imagine a safe place.

- A place just for you where you feel nurtured, safe and comfortable; a place of peace and serenity where you can completely let go.

- It can be a real or imaginary place.

- Allow the mind to effortlessly fill in the picture, without effort.

- Once you have a sense of this place, see if you can experience the environment as fully as possible. What do you see? What do you hear? What do you feel on your skin?

- Stay here as long as you like

- Know that you can come back here at any time. It is your personal place of peace and restoration.

EXERCISE — QUIET MIND
IN NATURE

Find one of these environments:
- The Sky (either at night or during the day)
- Pool of water (lake, ocean)
- Meadow or Valley

Find a comfortable position where you will not be disturbed by other people, cars, or other distractions.
- Observe the environment with a soft gaze.
- Do not focus on anything in particular.
- Allow the open spaciousness to fill your visual scene.
- Without effort, can you tune in to the gentle vastness?
- Allow the mind to fall into that space.
- Do not seek with the senses
- Just sit…being present and still

Note: you may also use a nature-based Virtual Reality meditation to facilitate this state. See Appendix 2.

EXERCISE — **RECEPTIVE PRAYER**
AS QUIET MIND MEDITATION

The word "prayer" often invokes an image of someone clasping their hands together at the foot of a bed and asking God for special favors or protection for loved ones. Receptive prayer is much different. Here's how it works:

Find a place where you can be quiet and undisturbed for a few minutes

Settle in to your posture, checking your body, breath and mind. Allow yourself to be fully present in the moment.

Ask for clear guidance. You may invoke someone or something of spiritual significance or you may invoke your Higher self (for example, "to my Higher Self, I ask for clarity, guidance, insight and psychological healing, please help me understand what I need to know right now.")

Let it go. Once you have asked for guidance, quiet the mind.

LISTEN. Not with your ears, listen with your heart. Quiet the small mind and practice receptivity. Simply listen without judgment or analysis.

Chapter 6 — What About **PTSD?**

PTSD: A SPECIAL CASE

You may have noticed that PTSD has been conspicuously missing from the mental health conditions targeted in previous chapters. This is not because the other practices aren't potentially beneficial, but because it is important to acknowledge some of the special challenges involved in working with trauma survivors.

Because many trauma survivors have a hyperactivated nervous system, you might imagine that the meditation styles designed to quiet the brain would be ideal. In fact, you will see and hear people specifically identify mindfulness and TM as techniques that can be helpful for trauma survivors. Such a statement is not false; it just needs a few qualifications.

MINDFULNESS AND PTSD

Bessel Van Der Kolk, one of the biggest names in the field of trauma treatment, states that "the core of recovery is self-awareness" (p. 208). He notes that trauma survivors frequently experience extreme sensations and often go to great lengths to avoid them. Of course, avoiding difficult feelings actually increases the likelihood that each occurrence of those feeling states will be overwhelming. It can become a self-perpetuating cycle in which a person goes to greater and greater lengths to avoid certain feelings or sensations. When those feelings inevitably arise, they are experienced as unbearable. This is a very logical and sometimes effective defense mechanism except that it does not provide the survivor with any skills around how to live with and navigate these difficult sensations.

At some point, it becomes important for trauma survivors to learn how to be present with their inner experiences; to learn to sit with discomfort or fear and recognize that such experiences are transient and do not last. It is important for them to recognize that they are safe in the present moment; that the events from the past or fears for the future are not actually happening right now. It is important to recognize the connection between thoughts and feelings; to discover ways that the mind is creating additional distress. However, this is advanced work and should be approached carefully with persons managing unresolved trauma.

MINDFULNESS AS A TRIGGER

For some, intentionally engaging in the experiencing of "being present" with thoughts, feelings and bodily sensations can lead to a resurfacing of unresolved issues and feelings. By itself this is not necessarily a bad thing, but for someone that is unprepared, does not have an appropriate level of support and/or experiences the resurfacing as overwhelming, this experience can trigger feelings of panic, spontaneous abreactions or flashbacks, re-traumatizing the survivor. At times, being mindful can leave a survivor feeling like they are trapped or helpless again.

This obviously presents a serious dilemma. Mindfulness is ultimately a useful and important skill for trauma survivors, but how do we know when and with whom to teach these skills without creating unnecessary distress? The short answer is that there is no definitive test. There is no foolproof way to know if teaching Mindfulness or Quiet Mind meditations will be "too much" for a particular client at a particular time. Fortunately, there are a few fairly straightforward guidelines to using these strategies with trauma survivors.

By providing informed consent, assuring appropriate support, regularly assessing the impact of the meditation practice, teaching skills related to grounding and titrating their exposure to mindfulness you can enhance the benefits and minimize difficulties.

INFORMED CONSENT

Anyone working in a mental health field will be familiar with the concept of Informed Consent. It is essentially making sure that the client has as much information as possible about their treatment. We tend to think of this as something that is covered at intake with accompanying paperwork. However, it is a concept that should be repeatedly addressed throughout treatment, especially with trauma survivors.

Informed consent is really about providing enough information to the client so they can make an informed decision. Because most trauma survivors have been in situations where they felt they did not have any control or where their control was taken from them, the therapist must take extra steps to assure that the client understands what treatment involves; the potential risks, benefits and process. If you use a treatment strategy that is less common such as EMDR, EFT or neurofeedback, the procedures involved need to be explained thoroughly.

How does this relate to meditation and mindfulness? If you are going to introduce these practices into your work with trauma survivors, the client should be provided with clear information on the following (at a minimum):

Potential risk: Engaging in mindfulness practice may put them in touch with feelings, thoughts and bodily sensations that are uncomfortable and distressing.

Right to discontinue: Survivors should be told explicitly that they can choose to discontinue treatment or the particular intervention at any time without any impact on your relationship with them.

Resources: If they decide to explore mindfulness or other meditative practices, how will they receive needed support outside of session? Will they have access to the therapist if needed? Are there other resources that could be available?

Grounding Skills: Before and during mindfulness practices with trauma survivors, it is important that they have learned and actively practice skills that help them manage their reactions when triggered.

EXERCISE — GROUNDING

Grounding is really a form of Mindfulness that directs the attention to the physical body or the external surroundings as a strategy to create distance from distressing emotional reactions. It is extremely important that grounding techniques are taught to trauma survivors during their early recovery, providing them with skills that allow them to have some control over their experience.

Grounding Basics:

- **Keep the eyes open:** remember we want them to connect to the present moment rather than getting pulled into memories or internal processes.

- **Connect to the body:** By feeling what is happening right here, right now, it pulls your attention in to the present moment and keeps you out of your head.

- **Belly Breathing:** breathing in a slow, rhythmic, consistent pattern from the belly signals to the body and brain that you are safe.

Grounding Strategies:

- **Describe the environment in detail:** use all your senses-what do you see? Smell? Feel? Say it out loud if possible.

- **Describe an everyday activity in detail:** How do you make a meal? How do you drive your car from your house to the grocery store?

- **Touch objects around you:** Notice the textures, size, weight, temperature, etc.

- **Move the body:** Jump up and down, push your feet into the floor, stretch, clench and release muscle groups.

- **Repeat a coping statement:** "I can handle this," "this feeling is only temporary," "I am safe now"

Adapted from "Seeking Safety" by Lisa Najavits (2002).

QUIET MIND AS A TRIGGER

Above, we explored the idea that intentionally paying attention to internal experiences (Mindfulness) could cause an increase in distressing feelings. This is pretty logical and straightforward, but I also mentioned that Quiet Mind meditations, such as TM, may also be problematic for trauma survivors. On the surface, this makes less sense. If distressing thoughts and feelings are the problem, wouldn't it be helpful to enter a state in which the mind is simply in a restful, quiet awareness; a state of "no thought?" Absolutely! Quiet Mind meditations could serve as a refuge; a wonderfully nurturing place of internal quietude. And, just like Mindfulness this may be a significant challenge or a trigger for survivors early in the recovery process.

In Chapter 5 we explored the way that Quiet Mind meditations tend to increase alpha1 brainwave patterns (8-10 hz). We also discussed how alpha brainwaves are associated with relaxation. The problem is that for many survivors, relaxing-letting your guard down—can lead to flashbacks, unwanted memories, or other forms of re-experiencing the trauma they have worked so hard to distance themselves from. The fact that relaxation can be a trigger is common knowledge among professionals working with trauma survivors. Because of this, special care should be taken when introducing any form of relaxation, including meditation. The client should have informed consent so they understand the possibility of intrusive thoughts or feelings. The client should have coping skills in the event they become flooded and the therapist should be skilled in the practice of helping someone become grounded if the experience is overwhelming.

RELAXATION: ACCESS TO THE SUBCONSCIOUS

On a surface level, we can understand that trauma survivors may be actively avoiding or distracting themselves from thoughts or feelings associated with the trauma. It is too painful to accept and so the mind creates strategies to keep this material out of consciousness. When the person relaxes, those strategies also relax and the images, sensory associations and bodily sensations can return, leading to an abreaction.

From a brainwave perspective, we can understand this process by considering the roles that brainwaves play in states of consciousness. In addition to the roles assigned to specific brainwaves in earlier chapters, our brainwaves are also associated with communication between the conscious and subconscious aspects of our mind. In this way, brainwaves play a significant role in the way that traumatic experiences are integrated (or not). By understanding this process in more detail, we can begin to consider meditative strategies that may be most helpful in the recovery process.

TRAUMA INFORMED CARE

A trauma informed response puts the survivor at the center of care. It is based on the recognition that many behaviors and responses expressed by survivors are directly related to traumatic experiences.

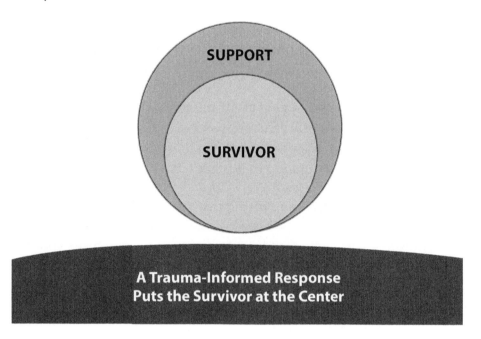

Examples of Trauma-Informed Approach

- Becoming knowledgeable about trauma and participate in ongoing training on how to offer trauma-informed support.
- Recognize that responses to trauma may include a numbing of feelings, a desire to avoid things that are reminders of previous traumatic experiences, and an increased sensitivity to these reminders, to people, and to the environment.
- Provide information to survivors about trauma and its effects.
- Offer flexibility and choices when possible as to how a survivor can interact with your programs and staff.

BRAINWAVES AND TRAUMA

Theta (4-8 hz): In addition to its role in ADHD and mindfulness forms of meditation, theta is also associated with the subconscious aspects of mind. The subconscious mind holds our long-term memories, aspects of creativity as well as suppressed psychological material. In her book, *Awakening the Mind*, (2002), Anna Wise describes theta as the brainwave state where you "hold your stuff." You can think of theta as a brainwave state involved in the programming of the mind. This is the brainwave state that is present when we are accessing or repressing material as well as during states of dissociation.

Beta (15-21 hz): These brainwaves represent conscious awareness and are dominant when we are engaged in active thought processes such as analyzing, planning, or problem solving. Beta is a fast brainwave and is often present in trauma survivors with hyperarousal symptoms. If beta is overengaged it can be related to things like anxiety and panic.

Alpha (8-12 hz): In the context of our current discussion, alpha is important as a bridge between the lower states of consciousness associated with theta and the waking state of consciousness associated with beta. Without alpha, you won't remember your dreams upon waking or have any recollection of your internal world during deep states of meditation. For information to move from the subconscious (theta) to consciousness (beta) you need a bridge (alpha).

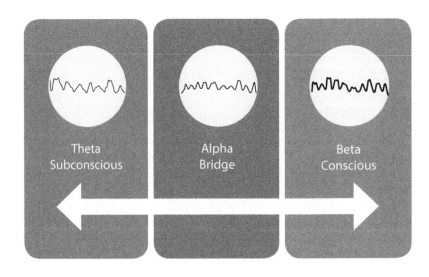

Theta
Subconscious

Alpha
Bridge

Beta
Conscious

THE PTSD BRAIN

Research and clinical experience indicate that persons diagnosed with PTSD may show one of several brainwave patterns. They may show elevated theta activity, elevated beta (Begic, et al., 2001) or decreased alpha and elevated beta (Begic, et al., 2003). These brainwave patterns make perfect sense given their potential role in states of consciousness.

Someone with excessive theta may be dwelling on memories (the past) or actively suppressing memories. Their subconscious programming may be dominating the conversation. This type of pattern may reflect situations in which an individual's unconscious beliefs, attitudes and fears are largely controlling their behavior but the person seems to have little/no awareness that this is happening. These types of symptoms are described in the DSM-V definition of PTSD very clearly and include intrusive symptoms associated with the traumatic event as well as avoidance of stimuli associated with the traumatic event.

We have previously established that someone with excessive beta activity may demonstrate difficulties with anxiety, sleep problems, and ruminations. Excessive beta can also be related to the other "marked alterations in arousal and reactivity" identified in the DSM-V, including irritability, reckless behavior, hypervigilance, exaggerated startle response, problems with concentration and sleep difficulties (DSM-V, p.272).

Where does alpha come into this picture? Alpha is the bridge connecting theta and beta. For subconscious material, including suppressed memories and intrusive images to enter the conscious mind it must move through alpha to get to beta. If you get rid of alpha, there is no bridge. For some persons with PTSD this appears to be a defense mechanism. On some level, they may believe that they cannot tolerate certain thoughts or feelings or memories; they may feel overwhelmed by certain internal states. The mind, in its effort to protect itself will block off those processes from consciousness. It will move the material into theta and minimize the likelihood of experiencing these things by significantly reducing alpha.

This appears to be a pretty effective defense mechanism. Unfortunately, like all defense mechanisms, it comes at a price. Because alpha is generally associated with feeling comfortable, relaxed and grounded in the body it makes sense that a lack of alpha could leave someone feeling agitated, anxious and uncomfortable in their body. How can we safely help trauma survivors rebuild that alpha without causing unnecessary emotional discomfort?

DEEP STATES: THE 5TH STYLE OF MEDITATION

A fifth category of meditative practice we will call Deep States, has received less attention in the research literature. This form of meditative practice shows great potential for working with PTSD and ironically shares some characteristics with Mindfulness and Quiet Mind practices. At first glance, it may seem that I am contradicting myself. After warning of the "dangers" of Mindfulness (theta) and Quiet Mind (alpha1), I will be promoting styles of meditation for PTSD that are characterized by alpha and theta!

The difference is that we will be intentionally using these deep states of consciousness to retrain and reprogram the subconscious mind. Rather than observing the distress or allowing the mind to be quiet and providing a bridge for all the buried trauma to creep into awareness, deep states training offers a different way to use attention and intention to promote integration and healing. Through the use of imagery, visualization and intention setting, the quiet and relaxed states of alpha-theta are used to promote integration of suppressed material and psychological healing.

Often, meditators utilizing these practices will be lying down or in a reclining chair with supportive cushions, pillows, blankets, bolsters, and eye masks. This form of meditation is focused on entering as deep a state of relaxation as is possible without drifting into unconsciousness. In fact, this type of meditative practice is literally a balancing act between relaxation and unconsciousness. Depending on the exact form of Deep States meditation, the meditator may spend time before the meditation imagining a desired behavior, feeling state or outcome. The meditator may also be guided during the meditation to experience an integration, a balance of opposite sensations, thoughts and feelings, helping the subconscious mind learn to manage and accept challenging internal experiences. This style of meditation has been predominately studied in two forms: alpha-theta neurofeedback and iRest Yoga Nidra.

ALPHA-THETA NEUROFEEDBACK

Alpha-theta brainwave training, sometimes referred to as the Peniston Protocol will typically begin with some form of peripheral biofeedback to assist in the relaxation process. Then the client will be guided into a clear visualization of the desired outcome just prior to beginning the session. The actual neurofeedback process takes place with the eyes closed and involves rewarding the brain when the person transitions between a dominant alpha brainwave pattern and a dominant theta brainwave pattern. These transitions are called crossovers and are thought to be an important element in integrating the subconscious and conscious minds. In essence, by dipping into the subconscious and then gently rebuilding the alpha bridge, it is believed that this process helps to reprogram the subconscious mind toward accepting a new and healthier reality.

From this perspective, this strategy shares some qualities with hypnosis. The subconscious mind (theta) is being accessed with the goal of helping to re-write some of the dysfunctional programming. At the same time, this process is significantly different from Mindfulness or Quiet Mind styles of meditation. With alpha-theta training the client is giving the subconscious mind input rather than entering a quiet state and observing the repetitious recordings already programmed into the subconscious mind.

Alpha-Theta as a style of neurofeedback began with a focus on chronic alcoholics that had not responded to traditional inpatient rehabilitation treatment programs. Using this protocol, Peniston and Kulkosky demonstrated an 85% success rate in eliminating alcoholic behavior in a treatment resistant population (1989). Following this initial success, the researcher/clinicians did similar work with Vietnam Veterans that had been suffering from combat related PTSD for more than 12 years. Compared to a control group that received "treatment as usual" including psychiatry and counseling, the alpha-theta group was much more successful. In fact, at 30-month post-treatment follow up, only 20% of the alpha-theta group still showed signs of PTSD, while 100% of the treatment as usual group showed continuing symptoms (Peniston & Kulkosky, 1991).

ALPHA-THETA NEUROFEEDBACK: **THE BASICS**

While there are many variations of this protocol, the general outline of treatment are outlined below:

1. Sessions 1-4: use peripheral biofeedback (e.g., skin temperature, skin conductance) and autogenic training to teach basic relaxation skills as well as orient the client to the biofeedback process.

2. Sessions 4-30:

   a. Begin with relaxation training utilizing skills from initial sessions

   b. Based on the client's needs/goals, create a visualization of the client engaging in a desired behavior, achieving a desired outcome, or avoiding an undesired behavior or outcome.

      • Ex: someone with alcohol dependence may imagine themselves at a social event where there is an open bar. They may imagine friends there drinking, having a good time and encouraging them to drink. They would then imagine themselves refusing the drink and feeling good about their will power, impulse control and decision making.

      • This visualization is clarified and repeated at the beginning of every session

   c. Alpha-Theta neurofeedback

      • Electrode placement is generally in the parietal or occipital lobes (e.g., PZ, P4, O2)

      • The client is generally in a comfortable chair

      • The room is quiet and dimly lit

      • Training is conducted with eyes closed for 30-45 minutes

      • Sounds are used to signal the client when their theta waves increase and become higher than the alpha waves (crossover).

   d. Wrap-Up

      • Following the neurofeedback portion of the session, many therapists provide an opportunity for the client to reflect on the experience.

         1. Discussion

         2. Journaling

         3. Drawing/Coloring

FUTURE DIRECTIONS FOR
DEEP STATES NEUROMEDITATION

The meditation and neurofeedback styles currently being used as a treatment intervention for PTSD generally seem to involve increasing theta brainwave activity which eventually becomes larger than alpha activity (crossover) as the intervention progresses. This work and these protocols are powerful and have been associated with impressive results with difficult clinical populations including alcoholics and those suffering with PTSD. Recent explorations into the study of consciousness has led to some new approaches and protocols for assisting clients into achieving altered states for the purposes of psychological and emotional healing.

Current research with psilocybin, LSD, DMT, and other psychedelics have all shown tremendous potential in treating a wide range of mental health disorders. It is believed that these impacts are due, at least in part, to the way these substances alter perception and the dysfunctional creation of a self-identity (Carhart-Harris, et al., 2012). Based on this emerging field, certain brain patterns and brain regions have revealed themselves as important in these transformative experiences. By targeting these brain patterns through neurofeedback, in conjunction with specific meditation strategies, we may be on the cusp of a brand-new approach to the use of neuromeditation for PTSD and other complex mental health concerns.

Heather Hargraves recently completed a proof of concept study demonstrating the potential usefulness of neurofeedback protocols that attempt to mimic the brain activation patterns seen in psychedelic research (Hargraves, 2017). She has also accumulated a set of case studies showing that consistent training with these altered states protocols can have significant and profound impacts on mental health functioning. The NeuroMeditation Institute is working with Ms. Hargraves to explore the various ways we might combine meditation and technology-based interventions to disrupt our self-imposed limitations and move beyond our small "selves," to a greater sense of health and wholeness.

Check our website (www.NeuroMeditationInstitute.com) for updates on this new and exciting application of NeuroMeditation.

IREST YOGA NIDRA

Yoga Nidra is an ancient meditation practice that is sometimes translated as "sleep of the yogis." It is a powerful healing method that helps meditators feel more connected to themselves, others and the environment (Miller, 2015). It does this by leading the meditator through sophisticated layers of self-examination and self-awareness.

YOGA NIDRA DEFINED

Yoga: the view, path, and means by which you experience your interconnection with yourself and all of life.

Nidra: changing states of consciousness, such as walking, sleeping, and dreaming, which include sensations, emotions, thoughts and images.

—Miller, R. (2015), p. 17

Richard Miller, a psychologist and long time student of Yoga Nidra, created a modern version of this practice with the name Integrative Restoration (iRest). This seems an appropriate name as the practice is designed to help people accept all aspects of themselves, becoming more psychologically balanced, healthy and resilient. The term "restoration" really captures the deeply nurturing state of rest that is encouraged during this practice.

At its most basic, iRest is a sequence of guided meditations that lead the meditator through experiences of body awareness and a "welcoming of opposites." This experience of accepting opposites of feeling and emotion, opposites of thought and opposites of bodily sensations appears to facilitate a true integration of the self. It is a tool to help the subconscious mind recognize that it is large enough to hold multiple and seemingly contradictory experiences at the same time. This process is healing at a core level and promotes an integration of unwanted thoughts, feelings and sensations. It is a safe way to reconnect with all parts of the identity and recognize that each of us are more than our pre-programmed beliefs and expectations. Over time, with continued practice, this meditative tradition appears to resolve many of the symptoms associated with PTSD.

At the time of this writing, two published studies have demonstrated the effectiveness of iRest Yoga Nidra with PTSD symptoms. The first was a qualitative study designed to examine the potential for iRest as an intervention with male combat veterans suffering from PTSD. After 8 weeks in the program, participants reported significant reductions in emotional dysregulation (e.g., rage, anxiety) as well as increased positive feelings (e.g., relaxation, peace, calm; Stankovic, 2011). A second study, conducted with female survivors of military sexual trauma found that 19 sessions of iRest over 10 weeks was effective in significantly reducing symptoms of PTSD, self-blame and depression (Pence et al., 2014).

TRAUMA INFORMED **IREST**

iRest Yoga Nidra is currently being offered in a range of formats. It is offered by yoga instructors and psychologists, in group and individual sessions, for personal growth and serious mental health concerns, and as an individual practice done at home with audio recordings and workbook. None of these are "good" or "bad," but each may have specific limitations based on the needs of the client. This was highlighted in a dissertation examining the impact of iRest Yoga Nidra on persons with complex trauma histories. While the participants in this 8-week experience reported positive impacts, many also noted important differences between practicing in the group versus practicing alone and difficulties linking the practice with life circumstances (Hartman, 2015).

Before recommending iRest Yoga Nidra to a client or someone living with PTSD symptoms, there are a few important considerations:

1. Training of the instructor: Does the person leading the iRest practice have appropriate training? Are they a licensed mental health professional?

2. Length of the program: Is this a single session workshop, a drop-in class for the community or a structured group for a specific population?

3. Available resources: Will the client have someone to process their experience with? What happens if they are triggered and/or have an abreaction during the practice? Is the client stable enough to engage in this practice without guidance?

CORE PRINCIPLES OF **IREST**

- **Learn to be welcoming:** Accept every thought, feeling and sensation just as it is.

- **Stop judging yourself:** Learn to think beyond "good" and "bad".

- **Know that everything is a messenger:** Every experience is information to be used in the healing process.

- **Accept what is:** Everything is as it should be in this moment.

- **Know that you're always doing your best:** We are all doing the best we can with what we have and where we are right now.

- **Understand the law of awareness:** There is power in simply noticing with a wide lens.

- **Discover your non-separate wholeness:** Recognize that you are more than your personality. You are whole, complete and connected to something greater than yourself.

- **Practice little and often:** Frequency of practice is more important than quantity.

From "The iRest program for healing PTSD" by Richard C. Miller, Ph.D., 2015

Chapter 7 — Putting It All **TOGETHER**

COMBINING STYLES

In this book, we have classified meditations based on four styles and how those styles impact the brain. As we have seen this is a useful strategy for considering how and why you might encourage clients to engage in specific practices. However, if you have ever attended a meditation in your community or listened to an audio recorded meditation, you will recognize that most meditations contain elements of more than one neuromeditation style.

For example, many meditations begin with focusing on the breath for several minutes and then transition into some other form of practice. This strategy is a way to help stabilize the mind at the beginning of a practice. As noted in Chapter 5, TM practices generally begin with a mantra focus (Focus), which is gradually replaced with a letting go and acceptance of quiet space (Quiet Mind). The Meditation on Twin Hearts for Psychological Health and Well-Being from the Pranic Healing and Arhatic Yoga traditions has 7 distinct sections of the meditation and each section impacts the brain differently.

This can make it somewhat confusing when initially attempting to apply the concepts in this book to already existing meditations. By understanding the intention behind each neuromeditation style, you can begin to explore and experiment with ways they might work together. They do not need to be mutually exclusive. They are presented as distinct methods for clarity and to help beginning meditators choose a style that best suits their needs and goals.

In fact, for many practitioners, it may be ideal to work with a meditation that combines styles. For instance, what if you take the NeuroMeditation Styles Inventory and two areas are nearly equal in their score? Or, what if Mindfulness is the primary style you identify, but when you sit down to meditate, the mind is running wild and it feels nearly impossible to notice what is happening in the moment? You may need to begin with a Focus practice to stabilize the mind. For this reason, Focus forms of practice are very often the first style that people are exposed to when exploring meditation. In many ways, the ability to focus the mind is a basic and critical skill to using the other meditative styles.

CHANGES IN GAMMA BRAIN WAVES DURING MEDITATION ON TWIN HEARTS:
STUDY ON NOVICE AND EXPERIENCED MEDITATORS

The Meditation on Twin Hearts is a primary meditation for Pranic Healers and Arhatic Yogis. In 2015, we studied one version of this guided meditation to examine the impact it has on the brain of advanced practitioners versus novice practitioners. Below is an examination of one of the key findings. Check out the research section of the NeuroMeditation Institute website for a full report.

Subjects were 12 advanced meditators with at least 1,000 hours of practice with this meditation and 12 novice meditators with no background in meditative practices

Subjects completed a range of questionnaires prior to the meditation as well as a 19-channel Qeeg and P300 recordings to measure brain response to auditory stimuli. Brainwaves were measured during the 30-minute audio recorded meditation. Following the meditation, subjects completed post meditation questionnaires, a post meditation Qeeg and P300 test.

The Qeeg data during the meditation was divided into 7 sections based on what was happening during that portion of the meditation. Some of these sections correspond very directly with NeuroMeditation styles which are identified in parenthesis below. These sections were labeled:

- Invocation (Open Heart)
- Prayer St. Francis of Assisi (Open Heart)
- Twin Hearts Meditation (Open Heart)
- Chanting OM (Focus)
- Silence (Quiet Mind)
- Chakra Healing (Concentration, Mindfulness, & Open Heart)
- Giving Thanks/Blessing (Open Heart)

The charts on the next page indicate the amount of change in gamma brainwave activity in the anterior cingulate during each segment of the meditation for both the novice and experienced meditators.

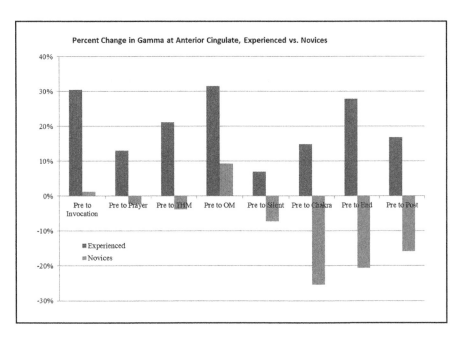

The above research is excerpted from the following study and presentation: Tarrant, J., Raines, N. & Blinne, W. (2015, Sept). Meditation on twin hearts and quantitative EEG: Study on novice and experienced meditators. 1st Annual Pranic Healing Research and Development Conference. Bogota, Columbia. To learn more about Pranic Healing and Arhatic Yoga go to www.pranichealing.com

This graph is showing the percent of gamma changes in the anterior cingulate from pre-meditation (baseline) to each segment of the meditation. You will recall from earlier chapters that the Anterior Cingulate is very much involved in focused attention tasks as well as tasks that require a regulation of emotion and cognition. This area of the brain is activated (increased gamma) during both Focus and Open Heart forms of meditation.

What we see in this graph is that the experienced meditators showed increases in gamma during every segment of the meditation. This makes sense as they have learned how to pay attention in very specific ways. Consistent with our expectations, the segments of the meditation related to Focus or Open Heart forms of practice showed the greatest increases. The two segments representing Quiet Mind (Silence) and involving a combination of multiple styles (chakra) showed the smallest increase.

For the novice group, they showed very little change in gamma during the first several sections of the meditation. The strongest increase was during the Focus portion of the meditation (OM). Interestingly, they showed significant decreases in gamma following this portion of the meditation. We suspect the subjects, being unaccustomed to this type of practice simply became very relaxed, resulting in a decrease in focus and reduced anterior cingulate activation.

PUTTING IT ALL TOGETHER TIP #1:   **WHEN IN DOUBT, BEGIN WITH A FOCUS MEDITATION**

In some cases, a person will not have a clear NeuroMeditation style or the identified style is too challenging for them at the time. In those cases, it is nearly always best to begin with Focus practices.

- Focus practices help a person learn to stabilize their mind and attention and very often results in a calming effect.

- Many meditation traditions teach this style to beginners before moving to more "advanced" practices.

- What if a person already has a fast brain pattern?

  o In general, you will not aggravate a fast brain pattern by practicing Focus meditations. . .., with one exception. I would be reluctant to teach Focus practices to someone with obsessive or compulsive tendencies

  o Many people with fast brain patterns also have difficulty focusing their attention. They are generally not "spacey" or daydreaming, but they can often get caught in thinking of too many things. Attempting to pay attention to too many things at the same time can result in attention problems, in which case, this practice can be helpful for them as well and serve as a baseline practice before engaging Mindfulness or Quiet Mind practices.

PUTTING IT ALL TOGETHER TIP #2:
ACTIVATION VS. CALMING MEDITATIONS

While this book has organized meditations into 4 styles, it is helpful to recognize that two of the styles have activating impacts (Focus and Open Heart) while two of them have calming impacts (Mindfulness and Quiet Mind). If you know through Qeeg brainmapping or observation that you have an overactivated brain, a combination of the calming meditations could be useful. Conversely, if you know you have an underactivated brain (depression, ADHD), a combination of the activating meditations could be beneficial.

ACTIVATING MEDITATION PRACTICES
- Focus practices increase Beta2 and gamma
- Open Heart practices increase gamma

CALMING MEDITATION PRACTICES
- Mindfulness practices increase theta
- Quiet Mind practices increase alpha1

WHAT FEELS RIGHT IS NOT ALWAYS THE BEST

It is common for meditation teachers, therapists and self-help articles to suggest that someone interested in trying meditation or meditation-type practices should experiment with a variety of styles and find the one that feels the best. This advice seems rather commonsensical until we consider it in light of what we have discussed in this book.

Consider my story: I began meditating in 1999 with virtually no instruction. At that time in Mid-Missouri, where I was living, there were no meditation centers or mindfulness classes. I largely just made things up until I was fortunate enough to locate a Zen monk living in my town. He was an instructor at the University of Missouri and held regular meditation sessions out of his home. I sat with him consistently for about 2 years and then on and off after that for another decade. He was a traditional Rinzai monk and our meditations involved ritualistic bowing and chanting of Japanese syllables and long periods of silent seated meditation. There were rarely any dharma talks or discussion about the practice. In fact, when I did ask conceptual or theoretical questions, the answer I received was, "Sit more." This traditional form of training discouraged thinking too much. Thinking just confuses the practice. Stop thinking and talking about it and just sit! The idea behind this style of meditation seemed to be to quiet the mind, not through effort, but by allowing the mind to find a state of "no mind;" reaching a place where the mind was quiet. I seemed to pick this up rather easily. It felt good and seemed to help me establish a more centered and grounded presence throughout my day.

This became my primary practice for many years. In fact, when I would sit with other groups or participate in retreats, I often resisted other styles of meditation. I disliked Open Heart forms of meditation. They seemed difficult and would often result in my falling asleep. It was like the words from the meditation instructor would wash over me and put me in a trance. I could not engage with the intent of the words as my mind was too relaxed; too quiet. This was the place I had learned to find in my practice and it was easy.

Years later as I became more involved in EEG neurofeedback and measured my own brain, I recognized that I had an abundance of alpha1 activity during baseline recording conditions. My brain was generating more than 3 standard deviations of alpha1 nearly all the time. I had read that alpha was associated with meditation and initially assumed all my meditation was paying off! My mind had entered a nearly permanent quiet place. Unfortunately, I was also experiencing periodic symptoms of ADHD, depression and narcolepsy. I found myself needing a nap every day, feeling fatigued and occasionally anxious. I knew from my work in neurofeedback that all those symptoms could be related to alpha activity. This is when the light bulb went off.

If my brain was already producing "too much" alpha1 and I was engaging in meditation practices designed to enhance this state, could I actually be making matters worse? Could meditation be bad for my brain?

Through some investigation I found that other researchers had already begun exploring the idea that meditation can lead to negative effects for some individuals. After all, if someone engaged in a meditative practice that moved the brain into the "wrong" direction, wouldn't it make sense that such a practice might create problems rather than resolve them?

In the research that went into developing the NeuroMeditation program I began spending more of my meditation practice in active forms of practice including Qigong, Taiji Chuan, Focus and Open Heart. In combination with some lifestyle adjustments I found that nearly all the "symptoms" I experienced years ago have vanished. On the next page is a Meditation Styles Self-Reflection that can act as a useful guide when preparing to undertake meditation.

The moral of the story: just because a meditation is easy, does not necessarily mean it is the best one for your brain. The Zen or TM style of meditation was easy for me because my brain already knew how to do it. It was comfortable. It was a mental state I could find without much effort, and it was also relaxing. It matched my idea of what meditation was supposed to be.

Clients need to know that anything worthwhile takes effort. If someone is engaging in meditation to re-balance his or her brain, doesn't it make sense that the practice might be difficult? It might be uncomfortable. If you are asking your brain to do something new; to change its old patterns, this is not likely to be easy. Meditation is work. It is not relaxation and it is not daydreaming. It is the re-training of the mind.

NEUROMEDITATION FOR PEAK PERFORMANCE

We have been focused almost exclusively on examining ways that this program can help with a variety of mental health concerns including ADHD, depression, anxiety, OCD, eating disorders, personality disorders and addictions. But what if someone doesn't have any significant mental health concerns? What if one is interested in meditative practices to prevent future problems, as a way to enhance well-being or as an avenue toward peak performance training? How does this information apply in those situations?

Rather than attempting to correct an imbalance in the system, peak performance NeuroMeditation involves using the same process to identify goals for achieving even higher levels of ability and performance. For example, an athlete may find that she becomes overly anxious during highly competitive situations causing doubt and leading her to make mistakes. By practicing mindfulness, this athlete can learn to watch her thoughts, feelings, and behaviors in an objective way; to detach from them and minimize their impact on her performance.

This athlete might discover that Mindfulness is the best match for their goals by taking the NeuroMeditation Style Inventory and looking at total scores or by looking at individual items on the survey to determine specific goals/interests that may not be reflected in the total score.

Another example may be someone in a romantic relationship who wants a deeper emotional connection with a partner. Again, after taking the NeuroMeditation Style Survey, this individual might find that Open Heart or Quiet Mind meditation styles are the best fit for that goal. And, this may be discovered by looking at either total scores or individual items.

WORKSHEET — **MEDITATION STYLES SELF-REFLECTION**

Ask Yourself the Following Questions:

1. Which meditation practices am I drawn toward? Why?

2. What does my current practice do to help my brain become more balanced? How?

3. Do I assume meditation should feel good? Why?

4. Do I avoid practices that are challenging?

5. How will I know if a practice is helping to balance my brain or not?

6. Am I engaging in practices based on my goals? (see NeuroMeditation Styles Inventory)

7. Can I recognize that meditation to rebalance the brain is working (with a significant payoff)?

8. Do I have myths around meditation?

   a. Meditation is supposed to feel good.

   b. Meditation is supposed to quiet the mind.

   c. People who meditate look and act a certain way.

More advanced practitioners may find that they have achieved a level of self-awareness that allows them to determine on a daily basis which style of meditation may be best for them on that particular day and for their particular set of circumstances. In this way, the information in this program should not be seen as somehow determining a single style that is best for someone's brain. Rather, it is a structure to help understand the impact of different meditation styles and then use that information to help shift someone into a place of optimal performance. Instead of looking at long-term goals of shifting overall states of arousal, it becomes focused on short-term goals and the question, what do I need right now?

PUTTING IT ALL TOGETHER TIP #3:
ACCESSORIES

Many beginning meditators want to do it right but they feel awkward and uncomfortable. They see pictures of beautiful people in yoga magazines with a full-blown meditation studio and get the idea that this is necessary to become an accomplished meditator. There is also an element of spiritual materialism that very commonly creeps in as someone decides to "become a meditator." There are all sorts of specialized cushions (zafus), mats (zabutons), bells, mala beads, Buddha statues, incense, music and clothes designed specifically for meditation practice.

- Have you ever avoided meditating because you "didn't have the right equipment?"

- What stories did you tell yourself? (e.g., "as soon as I get my meditation cushion. . .")

- When your meditation practice falls off, do you rely on the next accessory to help you?

- How many accessories have you purchased that you no longer use?

- Do you create stories about the accessories helping you to be more consistent or practice more efficiently or in some other way be a "better" meditator?

I would strongly encourage you to become aware of any stories you have created about the "right way" to meditate and recognize them as simply stories. Notice any ways that the mind is resisting engaging in the practice because you don't have the right equipment. Remember, the right way to meditate is about your state of consciousness, not your clothes or Buddha statue! The accessories are simply aids to assist in attaining a specific state of consciousness. Do not let your "lack of equipment" stop you from practicing.

NEUROMEDITATION STYLES INVENTORY
FOR PEAK PERFORMANCE

In many cases, the scores on the NeuroMeditation Styles Inventory will be enough to direct someone toward the best practice for their needs. However, in some cases, particularly when it involves a very specific goal, the total scores may not capture the best practice. In these cases, or in cases where all the section scores are low, it is better to examine individual items to identify the outliers. It may be that only 1 or 2 items on the entire survey have scores higher than a 3 and these can then be used to identify the best practice.

Example:

S. is on the swimming and diving team of their University. They are good, but consistently swim at a slower pace during competition than during practices. They recognize a tendency to get overly anxious during meets and worry that they will not do their best. S. has repeatedly received feedback from coaches that they need to "learn to relax" and "get out of their head." Friends and family have noted that they tend to take things too seriously. While functioning quite well in all areas of life, these perfectionistic tendencies have led to difficulties in work, school and social relationships.

S. completed the NeuroMeditation Styles Inventory and scored below the recommended cut off on all areas. No areas were identified. When comparing the 4 scores, they were all quite similar, none of them stood out from the others.

An examination of individual items revealed that two items stood out from the rest with scores of 5. These included:

- "When I have distressing thoughts, images or feelings, I am able to let them go" (Mindfulness)
- "When distressing thoughts or images pop up in my mind, I feel calm soon after" (Quiet Mind)

Based on this level of analysis, any meditative practices that lead to a quieting of the internal chatter or an ability to create distance from thoughts and learn to let go will be very beneficial!

NEUROMEDITATION FOR **SPIRITUAL DEVELOPMENT**

While not specifically designed to address spiritual needs, it is possible to think of the styles identified in this program as building on one another and leading to increased levels of spiritual awareness.

Focus: These practices form the basis and teach the practitioner how to stabilize the mind. This is necessary to successfully utilize any of the other styles.

Mindfulness: These practices teach the meditator how to begin disconnecting from the ego, the things we associate with our sense of "Self." This is necessary to recognize that you are more than your personality, a key step in spiritual growth.

Open Heart: Learning to become compassionate and empathic is the next step in moving beyond the "Self." This level of practice often leads practitioners to the understanding that we are all the same at a very basic level, including plants and animals.

Quiet Mind: This level is about letting go. Letting go of the self, letting go of the other. It is about recognizing through experience, not mentation that everything is connected and Holy. There is no separation. There is no "I." Everything is an aspect of God.

Appendix I — Learn more about NEUROMEDITATION

NeuroMeditation
Institute, LLC

If you are interested in additional training in the concepts and skills discussed in this book, there are several ways you might move forward.

First, visit the website www.NeuroMeditationInstitute.com. This site contains a tremendous amount of information, resources, basic and advanced trainings available all over the world. At this site, you will also find guided meditations for each of the styles as well as other helpful tools (including a computerized NeuroMeditation Styles Inventory).

TAKE A LEVEL 1 COURSE

The one day course titled, "Mindfulness-Based Interventions to Rewire the Brain" is based on the material covered in this book and provides an excellent introduction to the concepts and skills. This course is taught by Certified NeuroMeditation Instructors and serves as the basic didactic course required to become certified as a NeuroMeditation therapist. The courses are taught through PESI and provide 6.25 continuing education hours for most professions. Check the NeuroMeditation Institute website for locations and dates near you.

TAKE A LEVEL 2 COURSE

Level 2 courses are designed to offer an in-depth examination of each of the 4 NeuroMeditation Styles and provide a format to teach these classes in a 6 week format. The title of these courses include:

- Focus NeuroMeditation: Practical Strategies to Rewire the Brain for Increased Concentration & Self-Monitoring
- Mindfulness NeuroMeditation: Practical Strategies to Rewire the Brain to Reduce Anxiety & Stress
- Open Heart NeuroMeditation: Practical Strategies to Rewire the Brain to Improve Mood and Increase Empathy
- Quiet Mind NeuroMeditation: Practical Strategies to Rewire the Brain to Silence the Critical Mind

Each course is offered in a 1 day format throughout the year in a variety of locations. You can find workshops and register by following the links at www.NeuroMeditationInstitute.com.

EXPLORE EEG NEUROMEDITATION

One of the most powerful ways to practice the meditation styles described in this book is to do so while receiving direct information about the brain during the process. Because we know what the brain "should" be doing during each meditation style, we can measure this and provide guidance to the meditator, letting them know if they are "on track" and when the brain becomes distracted. This is the most direct and efficient way I know to teach people to find specific mental states.

You can find an EEG NeuroMeditation practitioner near you by checking the NeuroMeditation Institute website under "find a provider."

If you would like to provide EEG NeuroMeditation services to your clients, consider attending one of the NMI workshops offered through Stress Therapy Solutions. These

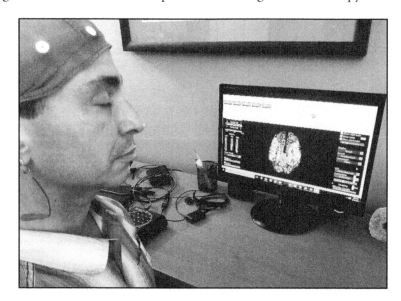

2-day hands-on seminars are designed for neurofeedback practitioners interested in incorporating NeuroMeditation into their practice.

BECOME CERTIFIED IN NEUROMEDITATION

Many therapists find themselves wanting more intensive training in the concepts and skills presented in this program. By becoming a certified NeuroMeditation Therapist (NMI-T), you will receive advanced training and receive mentoring from an NMI instructor. By completing the requirements for this designation, you will also become eligible to apply to become a NMI Instructor.

BECOME A NEUROMEDITATION INSTRUCTOR

After becoming certified as a NeuroMeditation Therapist and completing additional training, including serving as an assistant instructor with Dr. Tarrant, you will receive the designation of NeuroMeditation Institute Instructor (NMI-I), this will allow you to teach the Level 1 course throughout the world and provide mentoring for therapists seeking certification as a NeuroMeditation Therapist.

 **Appendix II** — **VIRTUAL REALITY** Meditations

As our preliminary research reveals (see Chapter 3), VR meditations can have an immediate and powerful impact on the person using it. Because the StoryUp meditations are done with real footage and take place in nature, the scenes are very calming to the nervous system and potentially provide additional benefit to the person experiencing it.

In conjunction with the NeuroMeditation Institute, LLC, StoryUP VR, is producing a series of nature based meditations that engage each of the 4 types of meditations discussed in this book. This becomes a very useful tool for home, work or school. These meditations also have a universal appeal and can be used by people of all ages.

If you are not familiar with Virtual Reality, it can seem a little intimidating at first. However, it is actually pretty straightforward and easy to use. In general, you need a headset, a computer (or phone), and software.

Unless you are heavily involved in video gaming, you will probably be using a stand-alone headset that uses your phone to run the programs. You simply connect your phone to the headset and the system is powered. The meditation software is available through StoryUP and can be purchased on their website.

So. . . to get started, you will basically need a phone (iPhone. . . or Android S6 or newer) and a headset. Phone based headsets cost about $100 and are available for purchase at large electronic stores (e.g., Best Buy) or through Amazon.com.

Once you have your gear, go to storyup.com on your mobile device for a link to download StoryUP's Iphone, Android and GearVR apps. There you will find everything you need to purchase the meditations and get them loaded on your phone.

Appendix III — **NEUROFEEDBACK** Resources

HOW TO FIND A NEUROTHERAPIST

If you are interested in trying neurofeedback or looking for a referral for a client, there are a few ways to find a qualified therapist.

1) You can simply search in your browser using keywords that include the name of your city (or a city nearby) and "neurofeedback" or "EEG biofeedback".

2) You can check out the provider listing at www.bcia.org. This is the only organization providing certification for neurofeedback practitioners. You can search by state and/or zip code. You will want to find a practitioner that is board certified in neurofeedback. They will have the initials, "BCN" after their name.

3) If you are specifically interested in neuromeditation, you can find EEG NeuroMeditation providers at www.NeuroMeditationInstitute.com

NEUROFEEDBACK TRAINING

If you are interested in learning more about neurofeedback and want to incorporate this into your practice, I recommend first considering equipment needs. Many providers entering the field of neurofeedback make the mistake of attending a workshop without first considering this question. This is problematic because most workshops focus specifically on one or another type of equipment and software. If you attend a workshop and decide you want different equipment, much of what you learned may not apply. The concepts will be the same, but knowing how to navigate the system will be a huge challenge. Also, different companies provide different capabilities.

Having owned many systems over the years, I am biased toward the equipment and software provided by BrainMaster Technologies (www.BrainM.com). As far as I can tell, their equipment provides the most versatility of any system out there. Meaning, you can do any kind of training with their system. This is the system I used to develop the EEG NeuroMeditation programs as it provides the capability of targeting deeper brain structures such as the Anterior Cingulate and the Insula.

If you have questions or concerns related to trying to figure out which system to purchase, please contact my office and someone can help you explore and understand the options.

Neurofeedback training that specifically uses BrainMaster equipment is taught through Stress Therapy Solutions (www.stresstherapysolutions.com). This training also counts toward becoming certified in neurofeedback.

Certification in neurofeedback is completed through the Biofeedback Certification International Alliance (www.bica.org). Check out their website for full details on the certification process.

References

For your convenience, you may download a PDF version of the handouts
in this book from our dedicated website: www.pesi.com/MeditationTarrant

INTRODUCTION

Farias, M. & Wikholm, C. (2015). *The Buddha pill*. London: Watkins Publishing.

Goyal, M., Singh, S., Sibinga, E., Gould, N., Rowland-Seymour, A., Sharma, R., Berger, Z., Sleicher, D.,

Maron, D., Shihab, H., Ranasinghe, P. Linn, S., Saha, S., Bass, E., & Haythornthwaite, J. (2014). Meditation programs for psychological stress and well-being: A systematic review and meta-analysis. *JAMA Internal Medicine, 174*(3), 357-368. Doi: 10.1001/jamainternmed.201313018

Holzel, B.K., Carmody, J., Vangel, M., Congleton, C., Yerramsetti, S.M., Gard, T., & Lazar, S.W. (2011).

Mindfulness practice leads to increases in regional brain gray matter density. *Psychiatry Research: Neuroimaging 191*, 36-43.

Kabat-Zinn, J. (1990). *Full catastrophe living*. New York: Bantam Books.

Rubia, K. (2009). The neurobiology of meditation and its clinical effectiveness in psychiatric disorder.

Biological Psychiatry, 82, 1-11.

CHAPTER 1

Cahn, B. R., & Polich, J. (2006). Meditation states and traits: EEG, ERP, and neuroimaging studies. *Psychological Bulletin, 132*(2), 180–211. doi:10.1037/0033-2909.132.2.180

Carter, O. L., Presti, D. E., Callistemon, C., Ungerer, Y., Liu, G. B., & Pettigrew, J. D. (2005). Meditation alters perceptual rivalry in Tibetan Buddhist monks. *Current biology, 15*(11), R412–3. doi:10.1016/j.cub.2005.05.043

Dunn, B., Hartigan, J., & Mikulas, W. (1999). Concentration and mindfulness meditations: Unique forms of consciousness? *Applied Psychophysiology and Biofeedback, 24*(3), 147–165. doi:10.1023/A:1023498629385

Goyal, M., Singh, S., Sibinga, E., Gould, N., Rowland-Seymour, A., Sharma, R., Berger, Z., Sleicher, D.,

Maron, D., Shihab, H., Ranasinghe, P. Linn, S., Saha, S., Bass, E. & Haythornthwaite, J. (2014). Meditation programs for psychological stress and well-being: A systematic review and meta-analysis. *JAMA Internal Medicine, 174*(3), 359-368.

Holzel, B., Carmody, J., Vangel, M., Congleton, C., Yerramsetti, S. Gard, T. & Lazar, S. (2011). Mindfulness practice leads to increases in regional brain gray matter density. *Psychiatry Research: Neuroimaging, 191*, 36-43.

Inanaga, K. (1998). Frontal midline theta rhythm and mental activity. *Psychiatry and Clinical*

Neurosciences, 52(6), 555–66. doi:10.1046/j.1440-1819.1998.00452.x

Klimesch, W, Doppelmayr, M., Russegger, H., Pachinger, T., & Schwaiger, J. (1998). Induced alpha band power changes in the human EEG and attention. *Neuroscience Letters, 244*(2), 73–76. doi:10.1016/S0304-3940(98)00122-0

Klimesch, Wolfgang. (1999). EEG alpha and theta oscillations reflect cognitive and memory performance:

A review and analysis. *Brain Research Reviews, 29*(2-3), 169–195. doi:10.1016/S0165-0173(98)00056-3

Lutz, A., Dunne, J., & Davidson, R. (2006). Meditation and the neuroscience of consciousness. In P.

Zelazo, M. Moscovitch, & E. Thompson (Eds.), *Cambridge handbook of consciousness* (pp. 499–554). New York, NY: Cambridge University Press.

Lutz, A., Greischar, L. L., Rawlings, N. B., Ricard, M., & Davidson, R. J. (2004). Long-term meditators self-induce high-amplitude gamma synchrony during mental practice. *Proceedings of the National Academy of Sciences of the United States of America, 101*(46), 16369–16373. doi:10.1073/pnas.0407401101

Rubia, K. (2009). The neurobiology of Meditation and its clinical effectiveness in psychiatric disorders. *Biological Psychiatry, 82,* 1-11.

Shapiro, Jr., D. H. (2008). Meditation: Self-regulation strategy and altered state of consciousness.

Piscataway, NJ: Aldine Transaction.

Travis, F. & Shear, J. (2010). Focused attention open monitoring and automatic self-transcending:

Categories to organize meditations from Vedic, Buddhist and Chinese traditions. *Consciousness and Cognition, 19,* 1110-1118.

West, M. (1987). *The psychology of meditation.* New York, NY: Clarendon Press/Oxford University Press.

Yogi, M. M. (1997). *Celebrating perfection in education. Maharishi Vedic* (2nd ed.). Noida, India: Maharishi Vedic University Press.

CHAPTER 2

American Psychiatric Association. (2013). *Diagnostic and statistical manual of mental disorders (5th ed.).* Washington, DC: Author.

Arns, M., Conners, C.K. & Kraemer, H.C. (2012, July). A decade of theta/beta ratio research in ADHD: A meta-analysis. *Journal of Attention Disorders, 17*(5), 374-83. doi: 10.1177/1087054712460087

Brefczynski-Lewis, J. A., Lutz, A., Schaefer, H. S., Levinson, D. B., & Davidson, R. J. (2007). Neural correlates of attentional expertise in long-term meditation practitioners. *Proceedings of the National Academy of Sciences of the United States of America, 104*(27), 11483–11488. doi:10.1073/pnas.0606552104

Brandmeyer, T., & Delorme, A. (2013, October). Meditation and neurofeedback. *Frontiers in Psychology, 4,* 688. doi:10.3389/fpsyg.2013.00688

Buckner, R. (2008). The brain's default network. *Annals of the New York Academy of Sciences, 1124,* 1-38. doi: 10.1196/annals.1440.011

Bush, G. (2010). Attention-Deficit/Hyperactivity Disorder and Attention Networks. *Neuropsychopharmacology REVIEWS, 35,* 278-300.

Castellanos F.X., Proal E. (2012). Large-scale brain systems in ADHD: beyond the prefrontal-striatal model. *Trends in Cognitive Sciences, 16*(1), 17–26. doi: 10.1016/j.tics.2011.11.007

Chiesa, A., Calati, R., & Serretti, A. (2010). Does mindfulness training improve cognitive abilities? A systematic review of neuropsychological findings. *Clinical Psychology Review, 31,* 449-464.

Clark, A.R., Barry, R., Bond, D., McCarthy, R. & Selikowitz, M. (2002). Effects of stimulant medications on the EEG of children with attention-deficit/hyperactivity disorder. *Psychopharmacology, 164*, 277-284.

Cortese, S., Kelly, C., Chabernaud, C., Proal, E., Di Martino, A., Milham, M.P., & Castellanos, F.X. (2012).

Toward systems neuroscience of ADHD: A meta-analysis of 55 fMRI studies. *American Journal of Psychiatry, 169*, 1038-1055.

Craigmyle, N. A. (2013). The beneficial effects of meditation: Contribution of the anterior cingulate and locus coeruleus. *Frontiers in Psychology, 4*, 731. doi:10.3389/fpsyg.2013.00731

Crottaz-Herbette, S., & Menon, V. (2006). Where and when the anterior cingulate cortex modulates attentional response: combined fMRI and ERP evidence. *Journal of Cognitive Neuroscience, 18*(5), 766–80. doi:10.1162/jocn.2006.18.5.766

Diego, M.A., Jones, N.A., Field, T., Hernandez-Reif, M., Schanberg, S., Kuhn, C., McAdam, V., Galamaga, R., Galamage, M. (1998, Dec). Aromatherapy positively affects mood, EEG patterns of alertness and math computations. *International Journal of Neuroscience*. 96(3-4): 217-224.

Draganski B., Gaser C., Busch V., Schuierer G., Bogdahn U., & May A. (2004). Neuroplasticity: changes in grey matter induced by training. *Nature. 427*, 311-312.

Jha, A.P., Krompinger, J., & Baime, M.J. (2007). Mindfulness training modifies subsystems of attention. *Cognitive Affective and Behavioral Neuroscience, 7*(2), 109-119. doi: 10.3758/cabn.7.2.109

Hasenkamp, W., & Wilson-Mendenhall, C. (2012). Mind wandering and attention during focused meditation: a fine-grained temporal analysis of fluctuating cognitive states. *Neuroimage. 59*(1), 750-760.

Huang, H., & Lo, P. (2009). EEG dynamics of experienced Zen meditation practitioners probed by complexity index and spectral measure. *Journal of Medical Engineering & Technology, 33*(4), 314–21. doi:10.1080/03091900802602677

Lehmann, D., Faber, P., Achermann, P., Jeanmonod, D., Gianotti, L. R. R., & Pizzagalli, D. (2001). Brain sources of EEG gamma frequency during volitionally meditation-induced, altered states of consciousness, and experience of the self. *Psychiatry Research: Neuroimaging, 108*(2), 111–121. doi:10.1016/S0925-4927(01)00116-0

Litscher, G., Wenzel, G., Niederwieser, G., & Schwarz, G. (2001). Effects of QiGong on brain function. *Neurological Research, 23*(5), 501–5. doi:10.1179/016164101101198749

Lutz, A., Jha, A.P., Dunne, J.D. & Saron, C.D. (2015). Investigating the phenomenological matrix of mindfulenss-related practices from a neurocognitive perspective. *American Psychologist, 70* (7), 632-658.

Lutz, A., Greischar, L. L., Rawlings, N. B., Ricard, M., & Davidson, R. J. (2004). Long-term meditators self-induce high-amplitude gamma synchrony during mental practice. *Proceedings of the National Academy of Sciences of the United States of America, 101*(46), 16369–16373. doi:10.1073/pnas.0407401101

Makris N., Biederman J., Monuteaux M.C., Seidman L.J. (2009). Towards conceptualizing a neural systems-based anatomy of attentiondeficit/hyperactivity disorder. *Developmental Neuroscience, 31*, 36–49.

Mason, M., Norton, M., & Horn, J. Van. (2007). Wandering minds: the default network and stimulus-independent thought. *Science. 315*(5810), 393-395. Doi:10.1126/science.

Monastra, V. J., Lubar, J. F., & Linden, M. (2001). The development of a quantitative electroencephalographic scanning process for attention deficit-hyperactivity disorder: Reliability and validity studies. *Neuropsychology, 15*, 136-144.

Okugawa, H., Ueda, R., Matsumoto, K., Kawanishi, K., & Kato, K. (2000, Oct). Effects of sesquiterpenoids from Oriental incenses on acetic acid-induced writhing and D2 and 5-HT2A receptors in rat brain. *Phytomedicine, 7*(5), 417-422.

Petersen, S. E., & Posner, M. I. (2012). The attention system of the human brain: 20 years after. *Annual Review of Neuroscience, 35*, 73–89. doi:10.1146/annurev-neuro-062111-150525

Pinker, S. (2012, January). 31 ways to get smarter-faster. Newsweek.

Ratey, J.J. (2008). *Spark: The revolutionary new science of exercise and the brain.* New York: Little, Brown and Co.

Schwarz, A. (2013, December 14). The selling of attention deficit disorder. *New York Times.*

Travis, F., & Shear, J. (2010). Focused attention, open monitoring and automatic self-transcending:

Wang, L., Li, W.G., Huang, C., Zhu, M., X., Xu, T.L., Wu, D.Z., & Li, Y. (2012, Nov). Subunit-specific inhibition of glycine receptors by curcumol. *Journal of Pharmacological Experimental Therapy, 343* (2), 371-379.

Categories to organize meditations from Vedic, Buddhist and Chinese traditions. *Consciousness and Cognition, 19*(4), 1110–1118. doi:10.1016/j.concog.2010.01.007

CHAPTER 3

Aftanas, L., & Golocheikine, S. (2001). Human anterior and frontal midline theta and lower alpha reflect emotionally positive state and internalized attention: High-resolution EEG investigation of meditation. *Neuroscience Letters, 310*(1), 57–60. doi:10.1016/S0304-3940(01)02094-8

Aftanas, L., Lotova, N., Koshkarov, V., & Popov, S. (1998). Non-linear dynamical coupling between different brain areas during evoked emotions: An EEG investigation. *Biological psychology, 48*(2), 121–138. doi:10.1016/S0301-0511(98)00015-5

Aftanas, L., Varlamov, A., & Pavlov, S. (2001). Affective picture processing: Event-related synchronization within individually defined human theta band is modulated by valence dimension. *Neuroscience Letters, 303*(2), 115–118. doi:10.1016/S0304-3940(01)01703-7

Babbage, Charles (1864). *Passages from the Life of a Philosopher.* Longman and Co. p. 67. OCLC 258982

Baijal, S., & Srinivasan, N. (2010). Theta activity and meditative states: spectral changes during concentrative meditation. *Cognitive Processing, 11*(1), 31–8. doi:10.1007/s10339-009-0272-0

Barks, C. (2004). *The essential rumi: New expanded edition.* Harper Collins Publishers: San Francisco.

Ba ar, E., Schürmann, M., & Sakowitz, O. (2001). The selectively distributed theta system: functions. *International Journal of Psychophysiology, 39*(2-3), 197–212. doi:10.1016/ S0167-8760(00)00141-0

Berto, R. (2014). The role of nature in coping with psycho-physiological stress: A literature review on restorativeness. *Behavioral Sciences, 4*, 394-409. doi:10.3390/bs4040394.

Cahn, B. R., Delorme, A., & Polich, J. (2010). Occipital gamma activation during Vipassana meditation. *Cognitive Processing, 11*(1), 39–56. doi:10.1007/s10339-009-0352-1

Cahn, B. R., & Polich, J. (2006). Meditation states and traits: EEG, ERP, and neuroimaging studies. *Psychological Bulletin, 132*(2), 180–211. doi:10.1037/0033-2909.132.2.180

Diego, M.A., Jones, N.A., Field, T., Hernandez-Reif, M., Schanberg, S., Kuhn, C., McAdam, V., Galamaga, R., Galamage, M. (1998, Dec). Aromatherapy positively affects mood, EEG patterns of alertness and math computations. *International Journal of Neuroscience*. 96(3-4): 217-224.

Dietl, T., Dirlich, G., Vogl, L., Lechner, C., & Strian, F. (1999). Orienting response and frontal midline theta activity: A somatosensory spectral perturbation study. *Clinical Neurophysiology*, *110*(7), 1204–1209. doi:10.1016/S1388-2457(99)00057-7

Dispenza, J. (2014). *You are the Placebo: Making your mind matter*. Carlsbad, CA: Hay House Inc.

Dunn, B., Hartigan, J., & Mikulas, W. (1999). Concentration and mindfulness meditations: Unique forms of consciousness? *Applied Psychophysiology and Biofeedback*, *24*(3), 147–165. doi:10.1023/A:1023498629385

Guzman-Gutierrez, S.L., Bonilla-Jaime, H., Gomez-Cansino, R., Reyes-Chilpa, R. (2015). Linalool and beta-pinene exert their antidepressant-like activity through the monoaminergic pathway.

Inanaga, K. (1998). Frontal midline theta rhythm and mental activity. *Psychiatry and Clinical Neurosciences*, *52*(6), 555–66. doi:10.1046/j.1440-1819.1998.00452.x

Kang, P., & Seol, G.H. (2015). Linalool elicits vasorelaxation of mouse aortae through activation of guanylyl cyclase and K(+) channels. *Journal of Pharm Pharmacology*, 67(5):714-719.

Kroenke K., Spitzer R.L., Williams J.B., et al. (2007). Anxiety disorders in primary care: prevalence, impairment comorbidity, and detection. *Annals of Internal Medicine*. *146* (5): 317-25.

Lutz, A., Brefczynski-Lewis, J., Johnstone, T., & Davidson, R. J. (2008). Regulation of the neural circuitry of emotion by compassion meditation: Effects of meditative expertise. *PLoS ONE*, *3*(3), e1897. doi:10.1371/journal.pone.0001897

McCraty, R., Barrios-Choplin, B., Rozman, D., Atkinson, M., Watkins, A.D. (1998). The impact of a new emotional self-management program on stress, emotions, heart rate variability, DHEA and cortisol. *Integrative Physiological and Behavioral Science*. *33*(2), 151-170.

Murata, T., Koshino, Y., Omori, M., Murata, I., Nishio, M., Sakamoto, K., Horie, T., & Isaki, K. (1994).

Quantitative EEG study on Zen meditation (Zazen). *Psychiatry and Clinical Neurosciences*, *48*(4), 881–890. doi:10.1111/j.1440-1819.1994.tb03090.x

Pan, W., Zhang, L., & Xia, Y. (1994). The difference in EEG theta waves between concentrative and non-concentrative qigong states--a power spectrum and topographic mapping study. *Journal of Traditional Chinese Medicine*, *14*(3), 212–218.

Selhub, E.M., & Logan, A.C. (2012*). Your brain on nature*. New York: Wiley & Sons.

Sapolsky, R. (2004). *Why zebras don't get ulcers, 3rd ed.* New York: Henry Holt and Co.

Shapiro, Jr., D. H. (2008). *Meditation: Self-regulation strategy and altered state of consciousness.* Piscataway, NJ: AldineTransaction.

Sherlin, L., Muench, F., Wyckoff, S. (2010). Respiratory sinus arrhythmia feedback in a stressed population exposed to a brief stressor demonstrated by quantitative EEG and sLORETA. *Applied Psychophysiology and Biofeedback*, *35*(3), 219-28. doi: 10.1007/s10484-010-9132-z

Spitzer RL, Kroenke K, Williams JBW, Lowe B. (2006). A brief measure for assessing generalized anxiety disorder. *Archives of Internal Medicine*, *166*, 1092-1097.

Wells, N.M., & Evans, G.W. (2003). Nearby nature: A buffer of life stress among rural children. *Environment and Behavior*, *35*(3), 311-330.

West, M. (1987). *The psychology of meditation.* New York, NY: Clarendon Press/Oxford University Press.

CHAPTER 4

Baehr, E., & Baehr, R. (1997). The use of brainwave biofeedback as an adjunctive therapeutic treatment for depression: Three case studies. *Biofeedback, 25*(1), 10–11.

Baehr, F., Rosenfeld, J. P., Baehr, R., & Earnest, C. (1999). Clinical use of an alpha asymmetry protocol in treatment of mood disorders. In J.R. Evans, & A. Abarbanel (Eds.), *Introduction to quantitative EEG and neurofeedback* (pp. 181–201). New York: Academic Press.

Berk, M. (2009). Sleep and depression: Theory and practice. *Australian Family Physician, 30*(5), 302-304.

Bratman, G.N., Daily, G.C., Levy, B.J. & Gross, J.J. (2015). The benefits of nature experience: Improved affect and cognition. *Landscape and Urban Planning, 138*, 41–50.

Brefczynski-Lews, J. A., Lutz, A., Schaefer, H. S., Levinson, D. B., & Davidson, R. J. (2007). Neural correlates of attentional expertise in long-term meditation practitioners. *Proceedings of the National Academy of Sciences of the United States of America, 104*(27), 11483–8. doi:10.1073/pnas.0606552104

Carson J.W., Keefe F.J., Lynch T.R., Carson K.M., Goli V., Fras A.M., & Thorp S.R. (2005). Loving-kindness meditation for chronic low back pain: Results from a pilot trial. *Journal of Holistic Nursing, 23*, 287–304.

Craig, A. D. B. (2009). How do you feel--now? The anterior insula and human awareness. *Nature Reviews Neuroscience, 10*(1), 59–70. doi:10.1038/nrn2555

Engstrom, M. & Soderfeldt, B. (2010). Brain activation compassion meditation: A case study. *Journal of Alternative and Complementary Medicine, 16*(5), 597-9. doi:10.1089/acm.2009.0309

Gilbert P, Procter S. (2006). Compassionate mind training for people with high shame and self-criticism: Overview and pilot study of a group therapy approach. *Clinical Psychology and Psychotherapy, 13*, 353–379.

Graham, L. (2013). *Bouncing back: Rewiring the brain for maximum resilience and well-being.* Novato, CA: New World Library.

Hammond, D. C., & Baehr, E. (2009). Neurofeedback for the treatment of depression: Current status of theoretical issues and clinical research. In T. H. Budzynski, H. K. Budzynski, J. R. Evans, & A. Abarbanel (Eds.), *Introduction to quantitative EEG and neurofeedback: Advanced theory and applications* (2nd ed., pp. 295–313). U.S.: Elsevier Inc.

Hanson, R. & Mendius, R. (2009). *Buddha's Brain: The practical neuroscience of happiness, love & wisdom.* Oakland: New Harbinger Publications, Inc.

Hofmann, S.G., Grossman, P., & Hinton, D.E. (2011). Loving-kindness and compassion meditation: Potential for psychological interventions. *Clinical Psychology Review, 31*(7), 1126-1132. doi: 10.1016/j.cpr.2011.07.003

Hutcherson C.A., Seppala E.M., Gross J.J. (2008). Loving-kindness meditation increases social connectedness. *Emotion, 8*, 720–724.

Ju, Y.J. & Lien, Y.W. (2016). Better control with less effort: The advantage of using focused-breathing strategy over focused-distraction strategy on thought suppression. *Consciousness and Cognition, 40*, 9-16. doi: 10.1016/j.concog.2015.12.002

Lutz, A., Greischar, L.L., Rawlings, N.B., Ricard, M., & Davidson, R.J. (2004). Long-term meditators self-induce high-amplitude gamma synchrony during mental practice. *Proceedings of National Academy of Science, 101*(46), 16369-16373.

Lutz, A., Brefczynski-Lewis, J., Johnstone, T., & Davidson, R. J. (2008). Regulation of the neural circuitry of emotion by compassion meditation: Effects of meditative expertise. *PLoS ONE, 3*(3), e1897. doi:10.1371/journal.pone.0001897

Lutz, A., Dunne, J., & Davidson, R. (2006). Meditation and the Neuroscience of Consciousness. In P. Zelazo, M. Moscovitch, & E. Thompson (Eds.), *Cambridge handbook of consciousnes* (pp. 499–554). New York, NY: Cambridge University Press.

Nair, S., Sagar, M., Sollers III, J., Consedine, N., & Broadbent, E. (2015). Do slumped and upright postures affect stress responses? A randomized trial. *Health Psychology, 34*(6), 632-641.

Nolen-Hoeksema, S., Morrow, J. & Fredrickson, B.L. (1993). Response styles and the duration of episodes of depressed mood. *Journal of Abnormal Psychology, 102*, 20-28.

Nusslock, R., Shackman, A.J., McMenamin, B.W., Greischar, L.L., Kovacs, M. & Davidson, R. (2007).

Frontal EEG alpha asymmetry in depression: The role of clinical state and emotion regulation. *Psychophysiology, 44*, S7.

Peper, E., & Lin, I.-M. (2012). Increase or decrease depression: How body postures influence your energy level, *Biofeedback, 40*(3), 125–130.

Phan, K.L., Wager, T., Taylor, S.F. & Liberzon, I. (2002). Functional neuroanatomy of emotion: A meta-analysis of emotion activation studies in PET and fMRI. *NeuroImage, 16*(2), 331-348.

Singer, T., Seymour, B., O'Doherty, J., Kaube, H., Dolan, R. J., & Frith, C. D. (2004). Empathy for pain involves the affective but not sensory components of pain. *Science, 303*(5661), 1157–62. doi:10.1126/science.1093535

Tarrant, J.M., Raines, N. & Blinne, W. (2015, Sept). ?*The Impact of Meditation on Twin Hearts On Psychological Functioning and Quantitative EEG: A Comparison of Experienced and Novice Meditators.* 1st Pranic Healing Research and Development Conference, Bogota, Columbia.

Tsai, H.-Y., Peper, E., & Lin, I.-M. (2016). EEG patterns under positive/negative body postures and emotion recall tasks. NeuroRegulation, *3*(1), 23–27.

Weng, H. Y., Fox, A.S., Hessenthaler, H. C., Stodola, D. E., & Davidson, R. J. (2015). *PLoS ONE, 10*(12), doi:10.1371/journal.pone.0143794.

Wilson, V.E. & Peper, E., (2004). The effects of upright and slumped postures on the recall of positive and negative thoughts. *Applied Psychophysiology and Biofeedback, 29*(3), 189-195.

CHAPTER 5

Berto, R. (2014). The role of nature in coping with psycho-physiological stress: A literature review on restorativeness. *Behavioral Sciences, 4*, 394-409; doi: 10.3390/bs4040394

Ciganek, L. (1961). The EEG response (evoked potential) to light stimulus in man. *Electroencephalography and Clinical Neurophysiology, 13.* 165-172.

Damasio, A., & Van Hoesen, G. (1983). Emotional disturbances associated with focal lesions of the limbic frontal lobe. In K. M. Heilman & P. Satz (Eds.), *Neuropsychology of Human Emotion* (pp. 85–110). New York: Guilford.

Edwards, B. (2012). *Drawing on the right side of the brain, 4th ed.* New York: TarcherPerigee.

Fehmi, L., & Robbins, J. (2007). *The open-focus brain: Harnessing the power of attention to heal mind and body.* Boston, MA: Trumpeter Books.

Jones, R., & Bhattacharya, J. (2014). A role for the precuneus in thought-action fusion: Evidence from participants with significant obsessive-compulsive symptoms. *NeuroImage: Clinical, 4*, 112–21. doi:10.1016/j.nicl.2013.11.008

Kaplan, S. (1995). The restorative benefits of nature: Toward an integrative framework. *Journal of Environmental Psychology, 15*, 169-182.

Kasamatsu, A., & Hirai, T. (1966). An electroencephalographic study on the Zen meditation (Zazen). *Psychiatry and Clinical Neurosciences, 20*(4), 315–336. doi:10.1111/j.1440-1819.1966. tb02646.x

Klimesch, W, Doppelmayr, M., Russegger, H., Pachinger, T., & Schwaiger, J. (1998). Induced alpha band power changes in the human EEG and attention. *Neuroscience Letters, 244*(2), 73–76. doi:10.1016/S0304-3940(98)00122-0

Klimesch, Wolfgang. (1999). EEG alpha and theta oscillations reflect cognitive and memory performance: A review and analysis. *Brain Research Reviews, 29*(2-3), 169–195. doi:10.1016/ S0165-0173(98)00056-3

Murata, T., Koshino, Y., Omori, M., Murata, I., Nishio, M., Sakamoto, K., Horie, T., & Isaki, K. (1994).

Quantitative EEG study on Zen meditation (Zazen). *The Japanese Journal of Psychiatry and Neurology, 48*(4), 881–890. doi:10.1111/j.1440-1819.1994.tb03090.x

Nakamura, R., & Fujii, E. (1990). Studies of the characteristics of the electroencephalogram when observing potted plants: Pelargonium hortorum "Springer red" and begonia evansiana. *Technical Bulletin of Faculty of Horticulture Chiba Univ., 43*, 177-183.

Nakamura, R., & Fujii, E. (1992). A comparative study of the characteristics of the electroencephalogram when observing a hedge and a concrete block fence. *Journal of The Japanese Institute of Lanscape Architecture, 55*, 139-144.

Takahashi, T., Murata, T., Hamada, T., Omori, M., Kosaka, H., Kikuchi, M., Yoshida, H. & Wada, Y. (2005).

Changes in EEG and autonomic nervous activity during meditation and their association with personality traits. *International Journal of Psychophysiology, 55*(2), 199–207. doi:10.1016/j. ijpsycho.2004.07.004

Travis, F., Haaga, D., Hagelin, J., Arenander, A., Tanner, M., & Schneider, R. (2010). Self-referential awareness: Coherence, power, and eloreta patterns during eyes-closed rest, Transcendental

Meditation and TM-sidhi practice. *Journal of Cognitive Processing, 11*(1), 21-30.

Travis, F., & Shear, J. (2010). Focused attention, open monitoring and automatic self-transcending: Categories to organize meditations from Vedic, Buddhist and Chinese traditions. *Consciousness and Cognition, 19*(4), 1110–1118. doi:10.1016/j.concog.2010.01.007

Ulrich, R.S. (1981). Natural versus urban scenes some psychological effects. *Environmental Behavior, 13*, 523-556.

Yogi, M. M. (1997). *Celebrating perfection in education. Maharishi Vedic* (2nd ed.). Noida, India: Maharishi Vedic University Press.

CHAPTER 6

Begic′ D., Hotujac, Lj., & Jokic′-Begic′ N. (2001). Electroencephalographic comparison of veterans with combat-related post-traumatic stress disorder and healthy subjects. *International Journal of Psychophysiology, 40*, 167-72.

Carhart-Harris, R., Erritzoe, D., Williams, T., Stone, J.M., Reed, L.J., Colasanti, A., Tyacke, R.J., Leech, R., Malizia, A.L., Murphy, K., Hobden, P., Evans, J., Feilding, A., Wise, R.G., & Nutt, D.J., (2011). Neural correlates of the psychedelic state as determined by fMRI studies with psilocybin. Proceedings of the National Academy of Sciences (PNAS, 109(6), 2138-2143, doi: 10.1073/pnas.1119598109.

Hartman, C. (2015). *Exploring the experiences of women with complex trauma and the practice of iRest-Yoga Nidra.* Doctoral Dissertation. California Institute of Integral Studies. San Francisco, CA.

Hargraves, H. (2017). Therapeutic Induction of Altered States of Consciousness: Investigation of 1-20Hz Neurofeedback. Masters Thesis. University of Western Ontario. London, ON, Canada.

Jokic'-Begic' N, Begic' D. (2003). Quantitative electroencephalogram (qEEG) in combat veterans with post-traumatic stress disorder (PTSD). *Nordic Journal of Psychiatry, 57,* 351-355.

Miller, R. (2015). *The iRest program for healing PTSD: A proven-effective approach to using Yoga Nidra meditation & deep relaxation techniques to overcome trauma.* San Francisco, CA: New Harbinger.

Najavits, L.M. (2002). *Seeking Safety.* New York: Guilford Press.

Pence, P., Katz, L., Huffman, C., & Cojucar, G. (2014). Delivering integrative restoration-yoga nidra meditation (iRest) to women with sexual trauma at a Veteran's medical center: A pilot study. *International Journal of Yoga Therapy, 24,* 53-62.

Peniston, E.G., & Kulkosky, P.J. (1989). Alpha-theta brain wave trainingand beta-endorphin levels in alcoholics. *Alcoholism: Clinical and Experimental Research, 13,* 271-279.

Peniston, E.G., & Kulkosky, P.J. (1991). Alpha-theta brain wave neurofeedback for Vietnam veterans with combat-related post-traumatic stress disorder. *Medical Psychotherapy, 4,* 47-60.

Stankovic, L. (2011). Transforming trauma: A qualitative feasibility study of Integrative Restoration (iRest) yoga nidra on combat-realted post-traumatic stress disorder. *International Journal of Yoga Therapy, 21,* 23-37.

Wise, A., (2002). *Awakening the Mind: A guide to mastering the power of your brain waves.* New York: Tarcher/Putnam.

CHAPTER 7

Brefczynski-Lewis, J. A., Lutz, A., Schaefer, H. S., Levinson, D. B., & Davidson, R. J. (2007). Neural correlates of attentional expertise in long-term meditation practitioners. *Proceedings of the National Academy of Sciences of the United States of America, 104*(27), 11483–8. doi:10.1073/pnas.0606552104

Lutz, A., Dunne, J., & Davidson, R. (2006). Meditation and the Neuroscience of Consciousness. In P.

Zelazo, M. Moscovitch, & E. Thompson (Eds.), *Cambridge handbook of consciousnes* (pp. 499–554). New York, NY: Cambridge University Press.

Tarrant, J.M., Raines, N. & Blinne, W. (2015, Sept). *The Impact of Meditation on Twin Hearts On Psychological Functioning and Quantitative EEG: A Comparison of Experienced and Novice Meditators.* 1st Pranic Healing Research and Development Conference, Bogota, Columbia.

Printed in Great Britain
by Amazon

Printed in Great Britain
by Amazon